2-Tone-2

Dispatches from the 2-Tone City - 30 years on

PETE CHAMBERS

In association with

Official book website at
www.myspace.com/2tonetwo

2-Tone, Coventry, 1979-2009

Introduction

The Rude Boys back together again, amazing stuff, who would have thunk it? What you will find in these pages, is a selection of 2-Tone 'happenings' over the last few years. Including some of my attempts to raise the bands profile, I apologise for sounding like some sort of 2-Tone warrior, I just happen to have the time to do these things, Sometimes it works, sometimes it doesn't. Some of the words in this book have made my Backbeat column in the Coventry Telegraph, some never did. The reunion of the band, kind of makes a lot of these previously unheard stories and unseen photographs far more pertinent now. It's almost become a kind of 'What we did on our holidays' scenario. It seemed a logical step to make these articles and photos available to all Specials fans everywhere. Because despite their absence there was always something with a Special slant, to write about, such is their legacy.

Many of you reading this will recall my previous 2-Tone/Specials outing, The 2-Tone Trail. That was our attempt to create the Specials brand visible and tangible in Coventry, the Two Tone City. For up to that point our best known, and best loved musical export had gone pretty much uncelebrated in its own city. Many ska fans have done the 2-Tone Trail, and it's a positive sign to see the trail, listed on the Coventry CV One site, as an official city tour.

So lets raise a toast to our heroes, it wasn't easy for them to do this, it seemed a lost cause, for so long, but they pulled it off. A huge thank-you must go to the Henry Kissinger of Two Tone Lynval Golding. He has been at this for over six long years. Just goes to show what can be done, if you grit your teeth enough! Praise of the highest should also go to all the other Specials, Selecter and 2-Tone people, for doing what they did then, and doing what they do now, respect to all you guys 'n' gals.

Some other Special people who should be singled out are Paul 'Willo' Williams and Mike Cornwell, more than fans of course, vital to the cause. Then there is Special Brew, they not only keep Coventry 2-Tone music alive, but their concerts are always 'happenings', and you never know who may turn up to play with them. You will see a face on the top left of the cover of this book, that gentleman is Darrell Johnson guitarist of Special Brew, he's there as a tribute to this band, who have taken the word Special and ran with it.

With Skanks

Pete Chambers

Foreword from Lynval Golding

For the 25th anniversary of the Specials, I had the dream of getting the band back together, I started the ball rolling then, and unfortunately it never happened. I never gave up though, and I kept pushing on, now it's coming to the 30th anniversary, we have to celebrate it in some form or fashion. We will celebrate the making of these records!

One person I would like to thank, more than anyone else is Pete Chambers, who has done everything to keep the band in the public eye. He's made sure we get played on the radio, more than any other guy, he's been keeping us alive through the media. When I talk to 17 or 18 year olds who know about the Specials, who did they learn from? They learned it from Pete, and all his writing, that's really helped keep our name alive. It's been an amazing trip, and the story of this book is a real story of the Specials. There's stuff in here, you won't see anywhere else. It lays down the places important in the bands history. The early places like Mr Georges, when we were the Hybrids, and the Coventry Automatics played before we finally became the Specials. Pete's a Coventry kid, and knows these places better than anyone, there's stuff in this book you won't see anywhere else.

Keep it Special

Lynval Golding

July 2008

Funny You Should Mention It!

Here is the article as published in the Coventry Telegraph spookily around the same time the Specials first began planning their reunion (October 2007) I put forward the case for a reunion, and against. OK The against part of the article, was written in the sense of fair play, I just put together some of the objections that had been aired over the past few years about why they could never work together again, from the heart, well put it this way, the first bit was.

Too Much Too Young

I'm a reasonable guy, I'm always keen to talk about local music, and answer the odd question when asked. You know the kind of thing, what was the first local hit? What is the best band to come out of Coventry? The one that I get all the time however, and I do mean, all the bloomin' time, is when are the Specials getting back together? How do you answer such a question? After all who knows? So I thought it's about time I addressed this most difficult of subjects. As it's not all black and white, I have decided to put up two arguments, for a Specials reunion and against a reunion. Make no mistake; this IS a tricky subject, especially to the former band members and the hard-core fans. The Specials website treats the word "reunion" as an expletive, and it's known only as "The Onion". This is just my take on it, and in no way represents the views of anyone else.

Yes, they should reform

Imagine the scene, it's the Ricoh sometime in the future. The Enemy have just encored with their third number one single, and left the stage to wild applause. Then a voice come over the PA, "Ladies and Gentlemen, for the first time in thirty years, please welcome home THE SPECIALS". The arena positively erupts, as Neville utters the words "Bernie Rhodes Knows Don't Argue" and history is made, and Coventry's finest are back where they belong, onstage together creating Two Tone magic to the emotional masses. Then sadly the alarm clock goes off, and it's time for more adventures in the 9 to 5 rat race. A dream it may be, but if those seven just men could put their differences behind them, then it would a glorious reality. How hard can it be? Ask about a reunion to the former band members, the chances are they will close ranks, and put up a united front. Avid Specials fan and Crystal Palace Chairman Simon Jordan, has supposedly offered 'silly money' to see the Coventry ska-boys reunited. The Specials answer to that is, "It's not about the money, and it never was". Honourable words, but these guys have put over a quarter of a century into Two Tone music. Their influence is worldwide, how dare anyone suggest they don't deserve some financial payback.

Something incidentally, they never really got in the eighties. These guys can't play forever, some day they will need some sort of pension. They totally deserve it, and if it makes them feel better, film the concert and give the DVD royalties to a charity of their choice. The fans are happy, the bands are happy and so are their chosen charities, perfect!

It's true that there is much animosity between the various parties, but when you see Roger Waters and the rest of Pink Floyd playing at Live 8, you know anything is possible. So I say, accept the fact that you don't all get on, and put your differences behind you for the greater cause. Roddy, Brad, Jerry, Terry, Horace, Neville and Lynval are all great blokes and musicians as individuals of course. Put them together though and they become one seventh of something much much bigger. They become a true giant of music, something iconic that belongs to everyone, and not just seven superb Coventry musicians. At the moment The Specials are still in vogue, with Amy Winehouse and Lily Allen covering their material, and they are still young enough to get on stage and do their stuff, albeit at a less vigorous pace. A few years on that may not be the case, I believe that deep down inside the boys would love to take that first scary step and bring one of the greatest bands back together, but only when the time is right, gentlemen the time is right, right now!

No, they shouldn't reform

The Specials created some great music in their time, it still of course exists on record, CD and video, so if you want to hear the band, you still can. So is it not better it stayed that way? Imagine if the band did reform, and the magic had gone, and instead of a glorious homecoming, we witnessed a parody of a once great band. Other problems that are bound to come up would be the fact that two of the band have full-time 9 to 5 jobs, and one of them lives on another continent for heaven sakes! As Horace often says, it wouldn't be like the Monkees, just pick up your instruments and play, it would take a lot of rehearsals to get that authentic sound back. Those of us who didn't tour with the band, will never know just how intense things got. I do know that Roddy Byers was deeply affected by the in fighting. So much so that he was unable to even listen to his own songs for many years. So telling Roddy to "let it lie", would probably cut little ice with him.

The Specials were a total product of their time; the post-punk landscape of the Thatcher eighties was looking for something fresh and vibrant. Then up jumps this superb seven-piece ska band with an appetite for the political and a black and white image to die for, perfect just perfect. Would it mean quite the same now? Their legacy is a proud one, not just for the boys in the band, but for our city too, how sad would it be to tarnish all that had been achieved. So let's not have a dawning of a new ERROR.

Photos by John Coles

Ray King-Two Tone Catalyst

Vibert Cornwall was born in St Vincent in the West Indies, though the people of Coventry will know him better as local soul legend Ray King! His talent as a soul singer is undisputed and without Ray Coventry's biggest musical phenomenon would never have happened, I speak of course of Two Tone.

It was 1966, when Ray (or Vibert as he was still then), first began singing in the clubs. "I decided to take singing lessons to improve my voice" Ray said, "I went to lady called Miss Kipper, paid my five pounds. She listened to me and told me to come back later. When I got back she gave me back my fiver and said I didn't need singing lessons as I had a natural talent. There was another lady with her, and she was a promoter and she agreed to get me bookings. So I had a photograph taken and played my first real gig at the Craftsman's Arms in Rotherham Road. I continued singing then I linked up with a band called Suzi and The King-size Kings". It was at this point Vibert Cornwall became Ray King and the group became the Ray King Soul Band. Their first gig was at The Walsgrave Club in Coventry, and from that moment everyone knew there was something special beginning!

Pharaohs Kingdom, the rare single from the band, issued under Ray's name.

9

Personnel Management:
John Tanner

Pharaohs Kingdom

Agency Representation:
Stateside Management & Agency
. Trinity House, 33 Trinity Street,
Coventry CV11BA (0203 23531/2)

walkerprint
London · ·

Pharaohs Kingdom, with (back row) Lynval Golding, Aitch Bembridge, Silverton and Desmond Brown. Front , Beverly Richards, Ray King and Laleen Barrett.

The bands reputation grew to the point when they were asked by the famous Playboy Club in London to perform. We had a vast repertoire of well-rehearsed songs we could call on. Owner Hugh Hefner was there as was Frank Sinatra, Sammy Davies Junior and Shirley Bassey. A real buzz went around. Hugh Hefner loved us and wanted us to reside for 6 months. We felt that was a little restrictive, as we wanted to play all over. So we agreed to play six months on, six months off".

The band continued to tour in Britain and Europe, eventually splitting up in the 70's. Ray was keen to put something back into music, so he started helping young bands. He knew the some black guys based in Gloucester Lynval Golding, Desmond Brown, Charley Bembridge and Silverton Hutchinson. Things weren't going too well for them so he brought them to Coventry and formed the band Pharaohs Kingdom with Ray on Vocals. Silverton introduced Neol Davies to the members of the band, he in turn brought along his friend Jerry Dammers, and with the inclusion of the Smith brothers a new band was formed called Night Trane. Ray took the band to Tunisia 'to get spirited', whilst in Africa Ray began toying with the Toots song 6th and 7th Book of Moses and it's ska beats. Back in the UK, they played for the first time at The Pilot, Ray wanted to go 'full on' ska but Jerry Dammers was not keen on the direction and left the band and formed what was eventually to become the Specials, Neol left too and would eventually form The Selecter.

Ray continued recording Ska, releasing the Micky Most produced "The Boys Are Back In Town" He went into management but continued to help the West Indian Community. "I began a Saturday School at the West Indian Club", reveals Ray. Some of the kids were kind of going astray. So we got a lot of kids off to University, of course being musical I helped a lot of kids in that department. I'm proud that many come back and thank me for sending them on their way.

Nite Train, with Neol Davies on right, and Ray king on vocals, plus the Smith Brothers (bass & drums), Jerry Dammers is on the Hofner organ obscured by Ray King. Picture from Neol's private collection.

11

2-Tone Celebration in Coventry

January 2006 I put a few ideas to my local BBC Coventry & Warwickshire, and this was the end result.

2-Tone's Coming Home

The eagerly anticipated 2-Tone Celebration centered at BBC Coventry & Warwickshire will be up and running from Monday 30th January. Everyone can get to hear at least some of the output via the website at www.bbc.co.uk/Coventry The Open Centre itself will play host to a series of classic 2-Tone photos taken by Toni Tye (www.tonitye.com) plus some interesting memorabilia from the late seventies early eighties (This is also being hosted at The Herbert in Coventry).

Monday 30th from 2.00pm Pete Chambers and a selected group will be walking some of Coventry's 2-Tone trail. From 8.00pm Pete will be talking to Coventry ska band Special Brew on Anita Miah's Evening show.

Wednesday 1st From 8.00pm Pete will be exploring the roots of 2-Tone with Amos Anderson on Anita Miah's Evening show.

Thursday 2nd A live event takes place from 7pm to 10pm with Liz Kershaw as host and featuring The All Ska's from Norwich, plus the debut gig from Neol Davies and Horace Panter's new band 3 Minute Heroes (with former Selecter man Aitch as guest drummer). Next up is Neville Staple and his band, and the night is topped off by Roddy Radiation's Skabilly Rebels.

Friday 3rd From 3.00pm the 2-Tone game show "You're Wondering Now" takes to the air, it features "The Judge Roughnecks" (Neville Staple, super fan Mike Cornwell and BBC Radio Presenter Clive Eakin) "Verses The Three Minett Heroes" (Horace Panter, Special Brew's Simon Kelly and BBC presenter Vic Minett). A recipe for *missing words* and *too much pressure!*

On the 2-Tone Trail at the Canal Basin for the BBC

Saturday 4th Author of The 2-Tone Trail Pete Chambers will be signing his books at Ottakar's Bookshop (located under the old Tiffany's site, now the library of course). With music from Gaz and Ronny part of Nuneaton's finest ska band The Tonics.

Sunday 5th Many of you have been voting for your favourite 2-Tone songs Now you can go back and vote on the shortlist on the site, the results will be revealed today (5th) on Vic Minett's ska Special from 2pm to 4pm.

Neville, Roddy, Neol and Horace at the BBC's Two Tone Live Event.

13

If the live show was the tops, then bubbling just under was the 2-Tone quiz, You're Wondering Now. It also went out live on Bob Brolly's afternoon show, in front of a live audience (which is always the best way, dead one's are much less fun).

There were two teams, The Judge Roughnecks who were captained by BBC presenter Clive Eakin and joined by ex-Special Horace Panter and superfan Simon Kelly, who is a member of the band Special Brew. The other team was captained by BBC presenter Vic Minett, so they had to be called the Three Minett Heroes. Vic was joined by Specials singer Neville Staple and superfan Mike Cornwell. The anoraks among you will wonder why Neville was not in the Judge Roughnecks as was the original idea, Vic insisted he be on her team, and so he was.

I set the questions, and was the official adjudicator, for what it was worth!

Below, Mike, Vic, Nev and Pete, bottom, Simon, Clive and Horace.

The Three Minett Heroes

The Judge Roughnecks

You're Wondering Now?
Here's a small sample of the 'easy' questions used in the quiz, how many can you answer correctly?

1. What is Specials Bass player Sir Horace Gentleman's real name?
2. True or False, Jerry Dammers was born in India?
3. In what location was the cover of the Specials first album taken?
4. Name the Two Tone band member who found fame in a cult Comedy Show?
5. Name the first Specials single?
6. What name would you find on Ranking Roger's birth certificate?
7. Which member of the Specials grew up in Kettering?
8. Who appeared on both sides of the very first Two Tone single, and on the very last?
9. The Kingston affair was better known as?
10. True or False, Roddy Byers once trained to be a priest?

That's just a small sample, they got harder, it was a great afternoon, lots of fun and some great insights into the world of the Specials thanks to Horace and Neville. The victors on the day were The Three Minett heroes.

Also part of the celebrations was the chance to vote for your favourite 2-Tone song, this is how it finished.

1 Gangsters - Special AKA
2 Ghost Town - The Specials
3 Too Much, Too Young - The Specials
4 The Beat - Mirror in the Bathroom
5 The Prince - Madness
6 Message to You Rudy - The Specials
7 Night Boat to Cairo - Madness
8 Missing Words - The Selecter
9 On My Radio - The Selecter
10 Tears of a Clown - The Beat

Answers to quiz. 1. Stephen Graham Panter. 2. True. 3. Coventry Canal Basin 4. Charlie Higson (of the Fast Show), from the band the Higsons. 5. A Message To You Rudy (Gangsters was under the name The Special AKA) 6. Roger Charlery 7. Horace Panter 8. John 'Brad' Bradbury drummed on the first single-Gangsters and The Selecter and on the last-Alphabet Army/ Al.Arm from JB's Allstars. 9. The Selecter, Gangsters 'other' side. 10. False.

Dear Diary

The best way to remember an event is look through your diary's, that's if you happened to keep one. Well sad as it may be, for many years I did keep a diary. I must say it's far from in-depth, but it does give some insight into the early 2-tone days from 1979 to 1981. The Ges mentioned is an old friend of mine, Ges Corbett.

1979

21st June– Buy Gangsters VS the Selecter, (probably from Virgin Records).
29th June-The Specials are in the Sun, national recognition at last!
6th July-(Dee a friend and graphics artist designs the first ever Specials badges on the planet. Ges wears one to see the Specials in Bournemouth, and gets to meet Elvis Costello).
19th July– See The Specials and Selecter at the City Centre Club, bloody magic night, Roddy nearly didn't get in, thanks to more than my jobs-worth security.
2nd August– Just seen the Specials on Top Of the Pops, they looked amazing, great for Cov all this.

The Badge that launched a million others

31st August-On Hols In Lloret, Spain, at Westender bar, asked the DJ to play Gangsters, and he did. We all danced and wore our badges with pride (even on my passport, how cool is that?)
22nd September– See Jerry and Neville Staples at the Dog & Trumpet, and talk to them, I end up giving Jerry my Cov ska Boys badge, great night.
2nd October-Just seen the Specials on The Old Grey Whistle Test, it's on again tomorrow, may get the tape recorder out!
8th November– The Specials, Selecter and Madness were all on Top Of the pops tonight, two tone rules.
29th November– Watch the Selecter and Specials at Tiffany's, about as good as it gets, both bands were superb, Pauline Black really rocks. That was until some bonehead bouncer attacks Ges for no good reason, we end up at Cov & Warwick A&E till 3.30. This ones for the bouncers.....
5th December– Just bought my tickets for the Specials gig at Tiff's on 20th, The Beat are in support, can't wait, hope the security is more tame this time?
13th December– the Specials are on TV twice tonight! (I don't say on what shows, but as it's Thursday, I guess one has to be TOTP?)
17th December– Up The Climax (pub), the band The Rest are playing, Sir Horace Gentleman is there, I get to talk to him, he seems a really nice bloke. He asks if anyone wants to come along on the Specials coach to the Rock Goes to College gig in Colchester on 19th. Ges goes, (I'm working so) have to miss it, s**t.

20Th December-The Boys (Specials), are back at Tiffany's, this time with the Beat, skank all night, two tone rules.

1980
19th February-The Selecter and The Flys are both on the (Old Grey) Whistle Test tonight!

27th February– Jerry and the boys win a Radio One award, they are in the States, Jerry speech begins says "What to say, I do not know" and John Peel makes DLT look an idiot. Well done the Specials.

12th March-Buy a copy of the paper Musicians Only, it includes a huge article about the Coventry Music scene, Coventry is the musical place to be, glad I live here.

20th March-Go to see the Specials, The Swinging Cats and The Bodysnatchers at Tiffany's. I don't get to see the Swinging Cats, Talk to Brad thought.

24th April- Madness play Tiff's, superb night, I find a Madness access all areas pass (and I still have it).

26th May– See The Swinging Cats on at the Hope & Anchor Coventry, great night.

25th September- Specials at Lanch, I have to miss this one, be there tomorrow though. (My lack of funds means I can only do one night. I only came out with £61 a week).

26th September– I go to see the Specials at the Lanch (and Swinging Cats), see Suggs in the upstairs bar. (I have my cameras with me and I'm wearing that Madness pass. I adopt an arrogant, "I have every right to be here" demeanour, and just walk through to back stage, taking all the photos I please. I recall I got so cocky, that I used one of the security mans shoulders to balance my telephoto lens on. Nev was at his best, clambering around the PA, great memories).

27th December-Over to the NEC Birmingham to see The Selecter, Madness, Squeeze, Rockpile, UB40 and Elvis Costello. Not bad, (so much for my finger on the pulse critique).

1981
3rd March-See Dance Craze at the Odeon, nice idea, but I expected more, don't know what though!

20th June–The Butts Rock Against Racism concert, had a great day out, loads of good bands. The Reluctant Stereotypes were spot-on. Hazel O'Connor was brilliant, she sat on the stage with her legs dangling, it was getting dark and she sang Will You, she was superb. So were the Specials, Ghost Town was a highlight. I take loads of photos, black and white and colour. (This would be the last time the Specials played in Coventry. There should have been more people there, but the ones who did attend witnessed a great feast of music. They also witnessed the demise of one of the country's finest bands. For as they played that night, at least three of the Specials had the name Fun Boy Three in their heads. A fitting finale I suppose?)

Teachin' Two Tone

2-Tone music has straddled the world, and it's always gratifying when someone other than a British subject acknowledges it. Enter American Professor Anthony Lis. Anthony was in Coventry as part of a three-week research trip investigating topics such as the connections between British folk music and American country music, Merseybeat and Brumbeat bands of the 1960s, and British ska and reggae for his classes; in addition to Coventry, Anthony also visited pop music-related sites in Liverpool, Birmingham, and London. Anthony teaches classes covering the history of country music and blues, jazz, and rock in the music department at South Dakota State University in the United States.

So why a visit to Britain? "Well you can get a lot of information on the internet, but there's nothing like meeting people in person, I visited the Herbert and viewed their Two Tone collection, in my class I talk about the song A Message To You Rudy, it was great to see the original 45RPM single there. They had an original publicity booklet from the earliest days of Two Tone, and in it they talked about the philosophy of the movement. The significance of the black and white symbolism, signifying not just the blend in the music but racial harmony too. Another publication that caught my eye was a booklet issued to promote the Two Tone film Dance Craze, as an American I hadn't seen it before and it was wonderful to see it list all the bands involved and what tracks they played. Also with my teaching there's something about when you hold the record, you remember that. It's a good to be able to relate memories from that particular record, or any record really. It gives you good fodder for teaching and coming up with things on the spot, it's part of your memory and you can draw from it. I believe that in teaching it's important to bring yourself into things, it makes it more interesting for the class, so trips like this are vital. So taking it back would be my primary source, beyond that I am not certain, but I have in my mind a follow-up trip already, to get even more focused on the British scene". I asked him why he visited Coventry in particular. "You see a lot of Americans are a little bit ignorant when it comes to Britain, I had heard about the bombing raids, but most Americans hear Coventry Cathedral they assume that's in London. I first started thinking about it separately when in my theory class they were doing something with the Coventry Carol. So I looked up the history of that song, it was interesting because they said it was from the mystery plays. So that got me thinking then I looked on the map, and realised it was quite a bit outside of London of course. I then heard a fellow teacher talk about ska music and it mentioned it was big in Coventry, so it was like, there's Coventry again so I had to check into it. Plus everyone I spoke to before my trip in Coventry was really positive and nice and it gave me a good feeling about the place, so it became a very important place for me to visit.

It's not all Two Tone however, Anthony originally trained as a composer; has become increasingly interested in the history of British and American popular music since taking over his university's pop music classes in the early 1990s. Related activities have included giving presentations on utilizing popular music examples in traditional college music theory classes and reviewing biographies of the blues singer Leadbelly and country and country-rock performers Porter Wagoner and Gram Parsons. "I was really surprised to learn of the British interest in country music", Anthony related, which he first became aware of when reconnecting with a friend from his graduate-school years in Ohio who now works for the BBC in London. "My friend, who was quite surprised to hear of my country music research (since when she knew me, I was totally absorbed with contemporary classical music) told me there was a 'huge following over here' for country, as evidenced by BBC producers specializing in the music, one of her colleagues fronting a constantly-gigging country band, and BBC1 producing their Lost Highway mini-series chronicling the entire history of the genre."

Professor Anthony Lis and a copy of The Specials Fan Club booklet.

Since then, I've learned of a recent book detailing the history of country music in Liverpool", Anthony continued, "while Pete (Chambers) has spoken of his father playing old Jimmie Rodgers recordings when he was young, echoing remarks made by recently-deceased Liverpool folk singer Pete McGovern that were offered on BBC Merseyside Internet radio last month - fascinating." Anthony's love of Coventry's 2-Tone ska, began when he first became acquainted with it when he purchased a CD for his Blues, Jazz, and Rock class that included the Specials' Rudy, a Message to You. "I sense a real energy and interest in trying new things on the best 2-Tone recordings", Anthony related, "like the A capella African-style singing that opens and returns towards the end of Nelson Mandela and the most-unusual chord progressions that underlie Ghost Town". Anthony teaches classes of 90 (yes 90!) 18 and 19 year olds, and you thought you had a tough job.

In the wake of his 2006 Coventry visit, Tony was asked by Leofric Films in Royal Leamington Spa to provide an interview for their "Ghost Town: 2-Tone Coventry Past and Present" documentary. In late-July 2006, after telling a friend from his hometown of Norman, Oklahoma about his 2-Tone research, Lis learned Norman had been one of the stops on the Specials 1980 American tour.

Lis's friend--who attended the concert, relayed that I'll never forget the concert the Specials sounded great, the band had their tonic suits, and I distinctly remember the vibe of the black/white aspects pushing and pulling the band. After about five straight punk tunes they lurched into a reggae feel it was awesome from there on in. During summer 2007 return trip to Coventry, Lis was pleased to learn that Horace Panter in his then-just-published Ska[1]d For Life: A Personal Journey With the Specials--devoted over a page to the Specials[1] Norman performance. (Tony was heartened to read Panter describe the gig as "storming" recalling the 600-plus Boomer Theatre audience getting up on its feet and dancing furiously to Concrete Jungle.

The administration at South Dakota State has been extremely supportive of Anthony's England trips, one administrator described his researching of materials for his Blues, Jazz, and Rock class as pertinent to the music departments goal of providing excellent introductory experiences for the general student population. Noting that scholars in England recognized Tony's knowledge in a way that brought significant positive exposure to the Music department. In December 2007, he was interviewed about his English activities in The Brookings Register newspaper, they printed an interview with him alongside a photo of him holding a photocopy of an early-1980s 2-Tone/Specials publicity booklet he obtained from the Herbert Museum in Coventry. Nice to see that Two Tone is truly global, and people in other countries hold it in such esteem as to teach it in their music classes, that's how important it really is!

Photo by John Coles

Making Movies

Out of sight is definitely not out of mind for The Specials. The longer they were away, the more people wanted to explore the Two Tone phenomenon. Rarely did a month go by in the last few years, without someone asking about the band, wanting to reform them or make a film about them! A couple of interesting local films about 2-Tone were Ghost Town by Leofric Films 2006, and an BBC Inside Out Ghost Town Revisited.

Ghost Town was a short documentary film investigating the Two tone brand in the city of it's birth. Supported by the Film Council, it was directed by Richard Wood and made by the Godiva Youth Gay and Lesbian group under the supervision of Paul Hardy. The project was funded by First Light Movies and Coventry City Council. Screenplay writers Ben-Elijah and JT Gareth.

The film features Horace Panter, Gaps Hendrickson and Amos Anderson, talking about the roots of Two Tone. Horace tells of how the Special learnt to play ska for the first time in the freezing cold at the Binley Oak. Playing essentially sunshine music in fingerless mittens. He also explained how the Coventry Council wanted to give the band a civic reception on their return from the USA. The band opted just to go down the pub and meet their mates. I did my 2-Tone Trail to camera, and the Skadigans played a great little ska song entitled Dance Around Like Zeberdee. all in all it came out very well. Far more professional than I could have imagined

The Author in Ghost Town , outside the Parsons Nose, attempting a piece to camera. With Paul middle, and Ben on Right.

BBC Inside Out is a local current affairs programme, usually picking three topics of interest, all usually unconnected. The Midlands edition decided to do a piece on Coventry and 2-Tone, entitled Ghost Town Revisited. For maximum visual impact they decided to recreate the Ghost Town promo video car ride. Long before the filming we met producer Lola Almudevar, at the Mail Box in Birmingham and in Coventry, looking for suitable sites. She was a lovely vibrant young lady, and on the day of filming she looked after everyone, and Neville in particular took a shine to her (no surprise there). Late November 2007 I learnt she had been killed in Bolivia in a car crash. So very sad, just 29, and a promising career ahead.

Anyway back to the day (21-06-06) we began early, the idea was to start pre-sunrise. By the time filming began, it had already begun to get light. The car needed to be fitted with the bonnet-Cam (I never heard anyone actually call it that, but just humour me here a little). Neville hadn't been to bed, so he was still tired, Roddy and Inside Out presenter Ashley Blake, got in the back seat of the

Spot the Bonnet Cam!

car. The car a cool Black Zodiac (Rodd had done a song about such a car, and took a shine to it) it was driven by the owner, who borrowed my hat to look the part. Myself and teacher and music fan Dave Barratt stood around, wondering why we got up so early. After multiple runs, they got what they were after, and we moved to The Ellen Terry Building, once the Odeon building. Dave and I got to do our pieces to camera, about Coventry, 2-Tone and the like. We moved down to The Parsons Nose chip shop, or at least outside of it (it has long gone). I'm always very aware when the topic of Ghost Town is raised by the media, you can bet your life, they are trying to create a Coventry ghost town of the early 80's. Racial problems, a bleak concrete jungle of a city. I felt that they just may be heading that way here, so I gave my usual rhetoric, about the fact it was a dichotomy, and while Cov was being thought of as a ghost town, it was in fact at it's artistic peak. Everyone wanted a piece of us, and every local muso' wanted to be the next local act to follow the Specials and the Selecter (not to mention Hazel O'Connor) into the charts. The place was actually buzzing. I said all this to the gathered blank faces. When I had finished a rather tongue in cheek Neville Staple and Roddy Byers suggested I should have saved that to when the cameras were rolling. S**t they were right!

Roddy and car, as cool as it gets

Neville and the sadly departed Lola

Other locations used were the canal basin, and Cardinal Newman Catholic School. It was here Dave Barratt came into his own literally drumming up a storm, with the pupil interacting, playing instruments even rapping. Nev and Roddy played a couple of songs, and gave the kids some sound advice in a Q and A session. Most of it not seen on the programme that went out of course, but it was a pleasure to hear two seasoned musicians who had been there and done it, talk so insightfully to a class of school children, who were trying to be cool, but seemed genuinely aware of just who was teaching them. It was incredible and a little inspiring to see Nev and Rodd approached by these young dudes, totally sussed with the Two Tone genre. Talking about songs and bands, that had demised long before they were born. More proof, if it were needed that the Two Tone legacy skanks on, indifferent of age or race. It was a long day and Nev had really had enough of the relentless interviews he and Roddy were facing. We finished late afternoon, but it seemed much later.

Ashley, Nev, Dave and Roddy and a very tired Mr Staple

Ska'd For Life-Mr Panters book

There have been countless books about the 'cult' of Two Tone music. Some good, some way off the mark. All of these books have been written by folks who knew the band, or just 'hung around'. That was until Sir Horace Gentleman released his own angle on things in the superb book Ska'd For Life.

I asked Horace what made you want to write the book and why at this particular time? "I'd always had this notion about writing a book about the Specials. I kept diaries when we toured in America and Japan and my parents bought the music press every week for the three years 1979-81 and had compiled 11 scrap books' worth of 2-Tone related articles, so I had a lot of source material to use. Plus I've got a pretty good memory. I started writing it after I had sprained my ankle and I was off work with nothing to do. It started out as a labour of love. I'm a schoolteacher these days so I'd pick it up during the holidays. It took about 7 years all told. I didn't try to get a publishing deal on it until 2005 and it was practically finished by then. I've spent the past 2 years re-drafting and editing it. The time scale is arbitrary, I didn't realise it would take 7 years. The tricky bit was getting everything in the correct order. I'd be walking my dog around the park and suddenly remember some ridiculous incident in a hotel in Barcelona or somewhere and rush back home dragging the dog behind me, so I could scribble it down before I forgot it. There was a lot of that sort of thing".

Horace at home, with his book and his bass

So what was the hardest thing/moment /experience to write about?
"The last year of the band's existence. Despite our fame and the success of Ghost Town, it was not a happy time for The Specials - which is why we split up. I didn't enjoy leaving the band but in order to maintain my sanity, it was something I had to do. It was not an easy decision".

Do you think this book will open up a can of 2-Tone worms?
"If it does, it will not have been me that has done it! The book was not written to embarrass or humiliate people concerning things that happened a quarter of a century ago, it was written to give my perspective on being in The Specials. I've tried to take a positive tone throughout. The only person I take the mickey out of is myself!"

Ska'd for Life: A Personal Journey with the "Specials"- By Horace Panter is published by Sidgwick & Jackson Ltd, ISBN- 9780283070297 priced £17.99.hardback and £7,99 Paperback. It's a must for all Specials fans, indeed one independent reviewer said of it, "Probably the best music biography I have ever read". So you can't say any better than that..

Above, H reading an extract at his book launch. Right a sneaky pic before they were ready and below H and coffee at a book signing at Borders.

Anthony Harty's Party 19th May 2007

The dictionary definition of party says, "a social gathering, as of invited guests for conversation, refreshments, entertainment". Well all of tonight's boxes were well and truly ticked, Especially the last box entertainment!

Anthony's musical career began at just 16, when he sent Paul Weller a demo tape of himself playing along to Speak Like A Child, within a few weeks Anthony became the bass player for The Style Council. He toured the world, with the band for two years. In 1987 joined the band The Truth, and did some more Stateside touring. It would take up too much column inches to list all the bands that this gifted musician has worked with, but here's a few, Coventry's Primitives, The Walnut Conspiracy, Duel, Badfinger, Beachmantango, The DT's, The Subterraneans, Box of Blues and the Specials and Beat Amalgam Special Beat. Not to mention playing on the Grammy winning Lee Scratch Perry album Jamacian ET.

So tonight's concert, oopps, sorry I mean party (it was actually a joint 40th, shared with Anthony's old mate Mark Quinney),was full of Anthony's old sparring partners. Various members of various bands, plus family and friends. The stage was set for action, Rog Lomas, as always the master of the mixing desk, worked his audio magic for the night. We were treated to some old Style Council tunes, followed by a full-on blues set from Neol Davies, Horace Panter and Anthony on drums AKA Box of Blues.

Re-Selecter, Pauline and Neol (plus Horace) back on stage, like no time had passed, a magical night.

Right, the multi-talented Anthony Harty

Uniquely Anthony is a multi-instrumentalist of the highest order, playing guitar, bass and drums. Not just a dabbler either, he actually teaches all three instruments! He's a pretty good vocalist too; don't you just hate people like that? So next we had The Truth (former Nine Below Zero's Dennis Greaves, Mick Lister and Rowan Jackson) working their way through an inspirational soul-set. Then it was Hazel O'Connor and the mighty Subterraneans (Anthony's current band) turn. I had the pleasure of seeing her the previous night at The Fletch, a superbly organised gig thanks to Phil. Now we were treated to Hazel and the Subs one more time. It was at this point I realised I was attending not just a party, but a musical tour of Coventry music. Who's Birthday was it again? Hazel as always was sublime, The Subs are her perfect backing band, more than a little evident in the delicious classic Will You. Last night Hazel described it as the love making song

(actually the Bonking song), tonight it had become the Tea and Coffee song (ironically as she swigged from a bottle of champers). This may sound cheesy, but each time I hear this song and Billy Davidson's perfect sax solo, it's like I'm hearing it for the first time, absolute perfection.

So we calmed down after Hazel's appearance, and did a bit more mingling, then we were sent to Two Tone heaven as Neol Davies and Horace Panter, with Anthony on drums, along with Justin on keyboards and Lee, Steve and Paul on brass took the stage for some reggae ska stylee. It may have escaped most peoples notice tonight when they launched into The Selecter (The Kingston Affair), that mixing the sound for this song tonight was Roger Lomas, the guy that originally produced this song that would find it's way on the first 2-Tone single along with Gangsters. Anyway just as I was about to take the grin off my face, Pauline Black got up on stage and like no time had passed between them. There were Pauline and Neol singing Train to Skaville and Too Much Pressure together again (too much pleasure more like). The Selecter were back, at least for tonight. A spot-on version of On My Radio followed, and still my grin refused to diminish. "It was probably the best moment of my life, said a rather happy Anthony Harty "it was just amazing, I was on another planet"! He's right, it was truly was an amazing party; I'm honoured to have witnessed it. Happy Birthday Anthony, can I stop smiling now?

New Kids On The Block are no Enemy

It would be an insult to artists like King, Fun Boy Three, Panjabi MC and The Primitives, to suggest that Coventry has made little impression on the charts from the decline of the Specials until the arrival of The Enemy. As someone who earns his money highlighting the impact of such bands, it would be naïve to dismiss them. On the other hand, there can be no mistaking the impact The Enemy have already made and how much it parallels that of the rise of the Specials. Make no mistake; this Coventry trio has made a fundamental inroad on its musical journey, which transcends any amount of hype the cynics may like to throw at them. These are the real deal, no question: Am I excited by a new Coventry band breaking on the scene? You bet I am.

Back in the late seventies, Coventry had little to shout about in musical terms, OK we had a great domestic history, but apart from Lieutenant Pigeon, Frank Ifield, Vince Hill and the Sorrows there was no real musical movement to talk of. However those of us who had witnessed the Automatics at Mr George's were the first to get a whiff of something-a-brewing on the local scene. Of course I'm not trying to pretend that what we had witnessed on those Monday nights was the 'real deal', it certainly wasn't. As the weeks went on though Dammers and Co perfected their brand of Ska we learnt was called Two Tone. By the time their first single 'Gangsters' was ready for human consumption, 2-Tone as a movement had begun, and black and white check was becoming popular.

The cream of Coventry musical talent. With members of the Specials, The Selecter, The Enemy and the Ripps. Plus Anthony Harty and Rog Lomas.

Single followed single, as hit followed hit, and Coventry it seemed had finally come alive.

Fast-forward some 27 years, and hey presto, and its Deja Vu time. Once again it's all eyes on Coventry once more. Like the city of the 80's, those eyes are not totally focused on the likes of just The Enemy and the Ripps. Having a successful rock band or two, can lift a city's musical reputation, much as a successful football team can. A&R people just can't help having a 'look see' at what else may be lurking in the back streets of Godiva's great city. In the early 80's, everyone wanted a piece of us with bands eager to record at Horizon Studios, just to get that Coventry sound. As the G Factor shows us there is no shortage of new talent right on our doorstep. Not all will become press darlings like The Enemy and there's another similarity; the Specials too could do no wrong with the likes of the NME and other 'finger-on-the-pulse' pop publications. As I write, the Enemy have two top tens singles to their name, and a number one album. Still the band has no problem wearing their Coventry-ness with pride, just like Nev and the boys of old.

The Enemy and The Ripps, along with members of The Specials and The Selecter were in attendance at the book Launch of former Specials bass player Horace Panter. It was amazing for someone like me to see the interaction between the old and new Coventry bands in the room. I asked Horace how he felt about it all. " It is very cool indeed to see a Coventry band in the charts again. It is even cooler when it is three spiky, angry young men who clearly have the word 'passion' written right through them. That's the impression I get from listening to their rather splendid album. The feeling in town reminds me of '79/80 when The Specials were happening. It seems everybody knows somebody who's related to someone from The Enemy. I'd wish them luck, but I don't think they need it". I asked Tom Clarke front man of the Enemy if he was influenced by the Specials at all? "The Specials are an indirect influence" he replied; "I was never a big Specials fan, however the lyrics of the Specials are as relevant to me and to anyone who walks through Coventry you walk 2 minutes down the road and walk up Far Gosford St and think of Ghost Town and it all makes perfect sense. So they were inspirational in the sense they were essentially saying the same as us. There are so many parallels; I was listening to Horace when he read a few pages of his new book about life on the road, and it was like he was describing the last 12 months of our lives. It was quite spooky, all the finest little details, like beginning in a little mini-bus then progressing to a tour coach, it's inspiring that there are so many parallels, so I have a massive respect".

The parallels of course continue, with the Enemy supporting The Rolling Stones at the O2. The Specials too caught Mick Jagger's eye once and the rock god wanted the Coventry septet for his own record label. Not to mention Neville singing 'Rudy' with the Enemy at the Colosseum in Coventry (this even made it onto vinyl).

he similarities go on and on. It's early days and comparisons will be made, retty soon though the novelty will wear off and when you talk Coventry music to he next generation of music fans it will be The Enemy they will mention on their wn merits, leaving just us old uns' the pleasure of knowing we got two bites of he musical cherry.

asked a few of the old brigade what they thought of The Enemy, here was their eplies.

Great band great name great songs great home town and one of them lives next oor to my sister Barbara, who is great too." **Neol Davies**

At last the baton has been passed from Coventry 's 2-tone movement to the next xciting and challenging musical generation spear-headed by The Enemy. I'm vith the lads on this one, because I'll live and die in this town too, if the music is his good"! **Pauline Black**

It is very cool indeed to see a Coventry band in the charts again. It is even cooler vhen it is three spiky, angry young men who clearly have the word 'passion' writ-en right through them. That's the impression I get from listening to their rather plendid album. The feeling in town reminds me of '79/80 when The Specials vere happening. It seems everybody knows somebody who's related to someone rom The Enemy. I'd wish them luck, but I don't think they need it". **Horace Panter**

I think The Enemy have the ability to be a huge musical phenomenon. I hope hey can stay grounded to their roots and I wish them every success and good uck.Of course, it is not going to be 1979 all over again...The Specials and Two one came from a time and a place in our social and cultural history. In the almost) past three decades, there have been enormous paradigm shifts and Coventry 2007 is a lot different from Coventry 1979. Nevertheless, it is great that fter all these years, another band full of youthful energy is helping to put the city nce more on the musical map". **Paul Heskett**

I saw The Enemy at the Coventry Godiva Festival and although I was very im-ressed with the band's energy & obvious songwriting talent. I don't think you can ven begin to compare their success with that of The Specials / The Selecter & he whole 2 Tone movement of 1979. Not to take anything whatsoever away from he Enemy, but 2 Tone was a lot more than music. It's message & fashion hanged peoples lives, hopefully forever ! That said, The Enemy have once more ut Coventry firmly back on the map, with dare I say it, virtually no help whatso-ver from the powers that be in Coventry (with the exception of CV One in en-ouraging local talent to perform at the Godiva Festival etc). The Enemy are like a reath of fresh-air again for Coventry & will hopefully turn out to be good roll mod-ls for other local bands following in their footsteps (watch out for The Ripps) " - Roger Lomas (Grammy Award winning Record Producer)

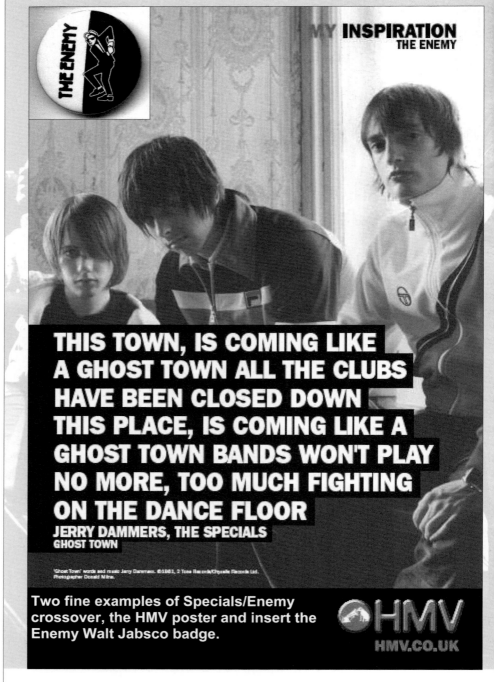

MY **INSPIRATION**
THE ENEMY

THIS TOWN, IS COMING LIKE A GHOST TOWN ALL THE CLUBS HAVE BEEN CLOSED DOWN THIS PLACE, IS COMING LIKE A GHOST TOWN BANDS WON'T PLAY NO MORE, TOO MUCH FIGHTING ON THE DANCE FLOOR
JERRY DAMMERS, THE SPECIALS
GHOST TOWN

'Ghost Town' words and music Jerry Dammers. ©1981, 2 Tone Records/Chrysalis Records Ltd.
Photographer Donald Milne.

Two fine examples of Specials/Enemy crossover, the HMV poster and insert the Enemy Walt Jabsco badge.

HMV
HMV.CO.UK

32

Ve'll Live and Die in these Ghost Towns.

On 3rd December 2007 The Enemy released the title track from their album We'll Live and Die In these Towns. Some hacks may want to compare the song to the Jam's That's Entertainment. Who cares, for this for many Enemy fans is the albums tour de force. It's lyrically superb, and paints a bleak picture of everyday life at it's 'ad infinitum' worst. With toilets smelling of desperation and a life slipping and sliding right out of view, it's a mighty finger-on-the-pulse epic that's brilliantly executed thanks to the musicianship of Holbrooks heroes Tom, Liam and Andy.

The band themselves are keen to point out that that the songs rational is not necessary a slight at Coventry or indeed any other town, it's more about standing up and being proud of where you live. Nevertheless the song has been well and truly pigeon holed as The Enemy's answer to Ghost Town. When the idea of a video to accompany the song was discussed, it was with typical genius from Tom and the boys who devised a clever pastiche based on the Ghost Town video. I recall a phone call a while back from Tom Clarke who knowing my love of all things Cov and music, suggested that I would appreciate the video idea they had come up with for the song We'll Live and Die In these Towns, and preceded to tantalise as he described that it would be a tip of the hat to the Specials Ghost Town video.

You may recall that video the Specials gave us to accompany the groundbreaking single Ghost Town. It saw our ska-heroes in sombre mood driving their way through empty London streets, an eerie video for an equally eerie song. Horace was driving, with Neville and Terry up front, and Roddy, Lynval, Brad and Jerry in the back.

The Ghost town video was shot in London late one Saturday night", recalls former Specials bass man Horace Panter,". It was June 1981 after an afternoon gig in Rotherham (See Horace's must-read autobiography for details - available in paperback Feb 08). We started about 9 in the evening and went on until about 8 the next morning. Quite a short video shoot by todays' standards. Quite an inexpensive one too. The car was a 1962 Vauxhall Cresta - three speed stick shift gearbox. We spent all night going back and forth under the Thames, The Black Wall tunnel with either a car in front of us filming, or driving with a dirty great big sucker stuck on the bonnet. One time the sucker came loose and the camera nearly rolled off the car. That bit was kept in the video. The guy who owned the car was less than pleased that we had marked his lovingly restored paintwork. As it gradually got light on the Sunday morning we headed towards the City, the financial district which was absolutely deserted and looked very spooky on the finished film. The end shots are of us throwing stones in the Thames".

Meanwhile back with The Enemy, like the Specials, our young rock stars are also in sombre mood, Tom sits in the back seat delivering the vocal line as Andy drives and drummer extraordinaire Liam Watts takes the passenger seat. As the song rolls out it's message of everyday boredom, the cities and towns may change, but the gloom remains. This video, like the Specials one some 26 years before, remains a perfect foil to a cleverly constructed and though provoking song.

Unlike the Specials, the Enemy take the Coventry connection one step further and the car they use is the former Coventry icon a Jaguar. On the road signs too Coventry is much in evidence as is Liverpool and Manchester. It's a great video but missing an appearance by one of the former Specials, that would have worked so very well, in the last frame Tom is replaced by a smiling Neville Staple But hey, you can't have everything!

TRIVIA As Horace has mentioned above, during the filming of the Ghost Town video a camera fell from the bonnet of the car, but the scene was left in. Those who have some time on their hands, will find the scene around 1.18 seconds into the song, look out for the zigzag light trail and the upward tilt of the scene.

New Kids on the Block-The Ripps

In July 08 I witnessed the Ripps making a glorious (and very hot) Headline return to the Kasbah, it was to be a Special night all ways around. For this Coventry Trio have tapped into the essence of 2-Tone, and in doing so, they have produced something very unique. They are currently recording their second album with the world's finest white reggae producer and Grammy winner Roger Lomas. What I have heard so far is incredible, and it's set to tick more boxes than the average census form when it finally hits the streets. So little surprise then that of late their gigs have begun attracting the local 2-Tone set. In attendance tonight to witness his new brand of ska, were former Specials, Lynval Golding and Horace Panter, former Selecter Pauline Black and Neol Davies, plus Roger Lomas and John Shipley from the Swinging Cats and Special AKA. It's all testament to this bands wealth of talent, and cross-genre appeal that gets the local muso's taking an interest.

If the Ripps had been around in 1979 they would undoubtedly have produced their records on the 2-Tone Record label, no question. This is a Coventry band that is capable of producing something new and fresh, yet still manages to tip their pork-pie hat to the Coventry Sound big-time. I asked Former Specials guitarist Lynval Golding what he thought of the Ripps? "I caught their rehearsal today, there is just three of them on the stage, but the sound was amazing. I may be a bit older now, but I have still got a bit of an ear for these things, so when I hear something that is right, I can spot it right away, and the Ripps have it. Sometimes it takes ten years or so for a trend to come back around, I'm afraid our trend is slow, but worth waiting for, and thirty years later here is the band that will take it to the next level. I believe" said Lynval. "That this is the band the baton should be passed onto, If the Specials get back, when the Specials get back this is the band that should be there on the bill with us".

The Ripps (Raul, Patch & Rachel), with Rog Lomas and Neol Davies.

I put this to the Ripps drummer Rachel Butt, "That blows my mind" she retorted "it's amazing, it's a wonderful compliment. There is a great 2-Tone influence, especially on the second album. With me rhythm-wise, I have always liked that kind of groove, and being from Cov and having that influence is just works so well together". I asked bassist Raul Lagunas the question that seems to be on a lot of people's lips, and that is, when is the second album coming out? "We don't have an official release date; we are hoping that something will happen before the end of September. We are pretty much there with the album, we have been working with Roger for a while and we like the set-up. We would like to get it out as soon as possible, but its those elements that have to be right like getting the right people behind it, and of course getting a label behind it. We have the finance in place and some options, so it really depends what out manager can do for us, at the end of the day the job is out of our hands". The band are well-known in their native Coventry of course, I put it to Raul on where the band stood as far as national recognition? "I think to a certain degree our name is out there, we have appeared in a lot of the cool, indie publication, and we have charted a few times in the Indie Charts. We have played all over the country and the album had some great write-ups so people into that scene know who we are". (Nationally many people heard the band when they played Glastonbury 2007; even more have heard them (albeit unwittingly), when their single Loco was used as the backing music for the BBC's coverage of England's Euro campaign.)

If the Ripps had been around in 1979?

The man responsible for innovating their sound is Roger Lomas, famed for his production of artists like Bad Manners, The Selecter and Lee Scratch Perry. I asked him what it was like working with the Ripps. "I can honestly say they are one of the easiest bands to work with, and that's out of all the bands I have done. Their ska direction is not down to me, that's the way they want their music to go. You see the easiest thing in the world is to make a ska sound of the past, with these guys I'm trying to create a new type of ska". Also in attendance (and right at the front with his head in a bass bin) was the driving force and main songwriter of the Selecter Neol Davies. "It's exciting times, they were excellent tonight, they are on the up, on the crest of a wave, I wish them every success".

They have some great new songs, many that include a brass section (for example the superb Daddy Was a Hero and The People Have Spoken), the future looks bright for this Cov trio I hope that by the time you read this the Ripps have become a big name.

Photos of the boys in concert, by John Coles, and right the hand written lyrics for Dawning of A New Era, From The Herbert Collection.

This is the dawning of a
new era
I met a girl from Area 3
She told me that she
worked in a chicken factory

This is the dawning etc
By 2 o'clock we were Brahms &
Liszt
I had to carry her home
through area six

This is the dawning etc
Sticks and stones may break
my bones
But in area six they throw
bottles and bricks

This is the dawning etc
We climbed the stairs to the
14th Floor
─ ─ ─ the key won't fit
the door

This is the dawning

A 2-Tone Friendly Coventry

OK, I know I keep going on about Coventry, and the home of Two Tone and we in the city should recognise this and recognise that. The fact remains, much as I love Coventry and its people, apathy can rule here a little too much. When Swedish furniture giants Ikea opened its doors in the city in December 2007, the papers were full of 'get a life' letter writers. Convinced that having a money-making mega employer in the city would somehow destroy the moral fibre of all we hold dear. That's the reaction you get from just a store, imagine getting interest from Mr and Mrs O.L.D Saddo, from Going Nowhere Avenue for 'just a pop group'.

Of course the Specials were never 'just a pop group', when I published the 2-Tone trail, I often wondered if anyone would care, or even worse, think I was trying to portray for Coventry and it's top band, a kind of Beatles/Liverpool scenario. A few thousand copies world-wide later, and hundreds of requests for more (and many fans actually coming here and taking the 2-Tone Trail). I am content in the knowledge that while I obviously accept that The Specials were not on the same level as the Fab Four (though to a lesser degree, the influence of Two Tone, like the Beatles has become global). The fact remains, while there are great fans out there curious to learn more about our native bands, we should promote what we have in this City, and more to the point be proud of it. I personally always get a thrill when I hear a Two tone fan describe Coventry as 'The Mother Country'. That's what this city means to some people, so have we moved on in the Two Tone promotion stakes?

So The 2-Tone Trail, The BBC's 2-Tone week, and Jerry's Honorary Degree aside. What tangible 2-Tone sites will a ska-mad visitor to Godiva's City find to use his brand-new 10 zillion mega pixle do-dah on? Hang on a minute, don't hurry me, I'm still thinking..... Oh, right, got one. Specials Urban art (never call it graffiti), in one of the city's subways (pedestrian underpass). Painted in striking red and yellow, this interpretation of a rather famous Specials promo photo. (See 'Out of Town Sites' in the 2-Tone Trail section.) Then we have the Specials own plaque on the Coventry Walk of Fame, outside the BBC in Priory Place.

Rodd & Hoz at the Walk of Fame Ceremony, Photo by Hannah Tobin, courtesy of BBC Coventry & Warwickshire

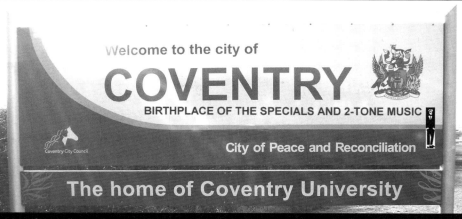

Welcome to the city of

COVENTRY

BIRTHPLACE OF THE SPECIALS AND 2-TONE MUSIC

Coventry City Council

City of Peace and Reconciliation

The home of Coventry University

ust a thought

'hen the whole thing is a farce, of course it wasn't a farce. Far from it, The Spe-
ials polled one of the highest votes from the people of Coventry, they voted for
ัem, and wanted them on their Walk of fame.

Vill we ever see a Two-Tone quarter in the City? Or will the welcome to Coventry
igns on the city's boundaries ever read Welcome to Coventry-The Birthplace of
`wo Tone? The movement is heading for it's 30th Anniversary, it's not just a 'pop
.and' anymore. This is one hundred percent social history, and it's all ours to
elebrate. In the future there looks to be a decent tribute to Two Tone in the mag-
ificent new Herbert project, I'm proud to be involved along with many others in
ัe creation of a temporary music exhibition at the Museum, that will hopefully
ัclude more than a little tip of the pork pie hat to the genre.

ัา Early April 2008, I was put in touch with Nick Stokes Director of Marketing and
Communications at Coventry University, by Councillor Tony Skipper. I talked to
Jick about celebrating the 2-Tone 30th and he was totally in agreement. I sug-
ested four 2-tone Trail plaques around the city. One outside Coventry University,
.ne inside the Library, one at 51 Albany Road and another at the Horizon Studios
ite. He agreed on principle to get them funded (see page 45). It's wonderful,
/hen the people who can make things happen, have the foresight to do just that!
`he same thing happened when I met up with Andrew Green, Head Librarian of
Coventry Library's. Not only was he happy to have a plaque in the building, but he
ad plans to surround it with a permanent display, showcasing the buildings his-
ɔry at The Locarno and later Tiffany's. better still, Neville Staple was in the build-
ัg that day, and there was talk of a live performance actually in the building!! It's
reat that these people really want to do something in this city, we need more of
ัem.

Doctor Dammers

In October 2005 I wrote a Backbeat Nostalgia column about the launch of my book, The 2-Tone Trail. In the article I looked at the impact of Two Tone music particularly in Coventry. I wrote, "That's seems to be the feeling of the time of course, the guys thought they were making music not history. Take 51 Albany Road, just a house that included a humble flat that included Jerry Dammers, a unique talent with a complete vision of what Two Tone was and what it could be. At Albany Road he defined the genre with the iconic 2-Tone man Walt Jabsco and made black and white check a fashion statement. More importantly along with the other 2-Tone bands, he helped to bridge the void culturally between black and white, and help fuel a movement that would see Nelson Mandela finally free. Yet as far as I can tell, he and the rest of The Specials and Selecter have never been honoured in their home city, no Honorary Degrees, no Freeman of the City. Seems a shame, of course I understand that they were just musicians, but what they created was more that just music, Two Tone was always more than just that. So maybe this book will help create a new awareness of the bands and their achievements in the city. That's why I'm reclaiming the phrase, "This town is coming like a host town"!

A little later on I got an e-mail from Kollette Super, the Associate Head of The Design & Visual Arts Department at Coventry University, requesting a meeting about the article. I was delighted to hear that they were very keen to bestow upon Jerry Dammers an honour degree! With my Coventry Telegraph article acting as a catalyst. I talked to Jerry just afterwards and broached the subject of honorary degrees with him. To my surprise and delight he said he would be happy to have such an honour bestowed on himself. So after months of me keeping silence, and lot's of work behind the scenes it is finally announced that Jerry Dammers would be conferred with an Honorary Degree of Doctor of Letters for his outstanding contribution to the international music industry on November 20th.

Jerry with Lynval at Coventry University collecting his honorary Degree

asked Kollette Super, why Jerry Dammers? "It was your Telegraph article that launched me into action" Kollette replied. "I knew that we had previously honored Pete Waterman and felt that Jerry Dammers had given both a political voice to that generation and a means of expressing their despair through his music both with the Specials and beyond that with 'Free Nelson Mandela' etc. I thought that it was important for us as a School to recognize the importance of the Two Tone movement to acknowledge its roots and the importance of the School of Art and Design in acting - sometimes- as a conduit for all these people to meet - and to the 'Lanch' in offering so many locations and venues. It seems that the Two Tone movement is valued and recognized world wide and I feel that this award goes some way towards honoring Two Tone and Jerry Dammers in the city of its birth. I think this award also belongs to so many it would have been good to recognize all the contributors individually".

So how does the man himself feel about the honour? " I really appreciate it, Said Jerry, "and I would like to thank whoever nominated me for this award, it's amazing really". I asked Jerry if it was a surprise after so many years? " I was a bit of a surprise, I wasn't of course expecting this". Last time Jerry gained a degree, he never attended the award ceremony to actually pick it up. I asked him what the difference was now? " Well I got the degree, but I didn't go to the ceremony for some reason, but it's nice to have a second chance". Jerry went on, "It's nice to get the degree from the University, but obviously Two Tone wasn't just me, by any means, there were a lot of other people involved. So I would like to thank all of them as well. It says in my letter they are going to present me with robes, so I'm looking forward to the robes". I suggested they might have some 'Special' black and white check ones on hand.

This of course is a massive step forward for Coventry music. The fact that a musical form, just a little over a quarter of a century old should be in consideration to be honored from the likes of Coventry University. Is great testament to a city that is un-blinkered and forward in its thinking, and prepared to recognize its talented sons and daughters from all walks of life. It is for me my number three in a five point plan to see Two Tone music given a higher profile in the city of it's birth. I believe that this award is not just for Jerry though, despite being the undisputed instigator of the Two Tone idea, he never did it on his own. There are 13 others who were responsible for the initial creation of the label and making this musical form a phenomenon throughout the world. They too must be remembered they are, from The Specials: Roddy Byers, Horace Panter, Neville Staples, John Bradbury, Terry Hall and Lynval Golding. From the Selecter there was: Neol Davies, Pauline Black, Arthur 'Gaps' Hendrickson, Compton Amanor, Charley 'H' Bembridge, Desmond Brown and Charley Anderson. Many others were also involved, but It was these fourteen people who created the fledgling 2-Tone record label, it's sound and it's cultural philosophy, effectively a blueprint that others would later work from.

A proud day for Jerry at Coventry Cathedral.

Lynval and Jerry at The Butts gig. Photo By John Coles

Photo by John Coles

43

Turning Japanese

The 2-Tone trail, (on advice from Neville Staple), went all oriental. I knew that 2-tone had a big fanbase over there, but was informed that although Japanese people tended to speak English quite well, they certainly wouldn't buy a book that was in English. So I had the main points of the trail translated into Japanese. It sold in CD-ROM form. We had some interest, and the local tourist office stocked it, it created a lot of publicity, but I can't really say that it was big in Japan though!

Neville, The Author and Roddy turning Japanese! Below the cover Nippon stylee!

ピーター・チェインバーズ著

ツートーン の軌跡

ツートーン コベントリー決定版ガイド

The 2-Tone Trail
by Pete Chambers

The definitive guide to Two Tone Coventry

Foreword by Neol Davies of The Selecter

Future Developments?

As I write, we approach the 30th Anniversary of 2-Tone. We are doing all we can to 'big-up' the event in Coventry. It's only right and proper we do something special' to commemorate the anniversary. One project that looks to be a goer, is the sighting of four 2-Tone Trail plaques around the city. Below is a rough idea, of what they will look like, and their locations.

Coventry University (The Lanch)

The Horizon Studio Site

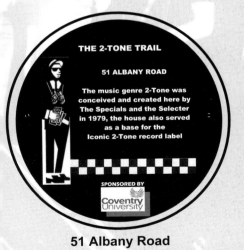

51 Albany Road

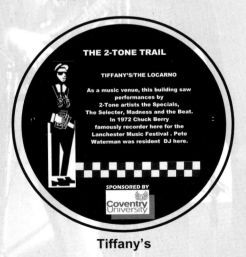

Tiffany's

The always obliging Nev, holds up a artists impression (basically my tatty attempt) of what the plaques may look like in Central Library, formerly Tiffany's. Right, Nev takes his library books back, actually he's looking at what 2-tone books the library has to offer.

Photo by John Coles

Photo by John Coles

2-Tone@30

"Well it was thirty years ago today, Jerry Dammers got the band to play". Amazing isn't it, thirty years, that makes it a pearl anniversary, maybe we should all go to Pearls cafe to celebrate then? But seriously folks, I asked a number of 2-Tone people about 2-Tone thirty years on, what it meant to them, it's legacy and their proudest moment. So here goes.....

CHARLEY 'AITCH' BEMBRIDGE-THE SELECTER

It's been a long haul, and I just wish that what 2-tone meant then, there would be more of togetherness now than a separation. Thirty years ago, we were all young, happy and wanted to play music. From the business point of view the wool was pulled over our eyes. I just wish that people could come together and talk and make amends. My proudest memory of 2-Tone was actually getting out there, being established, doing TV work all that kind of stuff and actually getting the band into the limelight. We had something very powerful, and it's taken thirty years for us to realise just how powerful it really was! An amazing time of my life, and we became part of history, it was a proud moment to have all these people together at one time, doing something positive together.

ROGER LOMAS-2-TONE PRODUCER

As I produced one side of the very first 2 TONE single ("The Selecter" - by 'The Selecter' on the other side of "Gangsters" - by 'The Specials') the 30th anniversary of 2 TONE obviously means a great deal to me (although for me personally, & I'm sure, Neol Davies of 'The Selecter', the real 30th anniversary for us was 1977 - the year that we recorded "The Selecter") The main significance, I suppose, is that 2 TONE has become much more than just a record label ... it is now seen worldwide as a style of music in it's own right by being branded as '2 TONE SKA' .

The main relevance of 2 TONE, certainly in Coventry, is that certain bands in the city (who were not even born in 1979 when it all started) are influenced by the 2 TONE bands & have managed to adapt the feel & spirit of 2 TONE along with their own music to form a sort of 'New Ska' which I am very much in favour of. My proudest moment was in March 1980 when I had three singles in the top 30 ... & all three bands appeared on Top Of The Pops on the same night 'The Selecter' with "Missing Words" ... 'Bad Manners' with "Ne-Ne Na-Na Na-Na Nu-Nu" .. & 'The Bodysnatchers' with "Let's Do Rock Steady".

DAVE WAKELING-THE BEAT

I can't believe we did 2-Tone in the first place, and I can't believe it was that long ago. I'm still waiting for most of us to grow up. I think it has become far more sig-

nificant than anybody might have guessed. I live here in America, we just played a gig near Boston, and there's a huge teenage ska scene there. As Lynval found out when he sat in with us a couple of months ago, as the Specials are kind of Demigods here.

I think 2-Tone was it was a lot of things, it wasn't just the music, it was the idea of an independent record company with its own label. Us on the inside found out that having a boutique label on a major, didn't really give you inde-pendence, it just looked like it in the glossy magazines. I think more than anything else, it was the historical timing of 2-Tone making statements about people of different colour and being able to get on with each other. I think it was incredibly well timed. It took a lot of steam out of the National Front and The British Movement's attempt to start a race-war in Britain. I think that was well done, and I don't think it was ever set about to be a conscious thing. It came out as genuine and natural from the musicians, and seemed to resonate with the population. Because of the fact it was genuine, it's gone into the history books of something of tremendous value.

I think my proudest 2-Tone moment was getting on the front of Face Magazine, with a borrowed sheepskin jacket, and a bit of Mars Bar wrapper over my front two teeth-Jerry Dammers! One of my other proudest moments was coming from Birmingham actually getting on with the people from Coventry! Me and Lynval joke about it, and if people from Birmingham and Coventry can get on then every-body can get on!

Would there be any chance of you and Ranking Roger doing anything to-gether? I have been inviting him for ages; he's just playing silly buggers. I have no problem with Roger at all. My take is, one hears little stories of the Specials getting back together, frankly I think it's what the fans think of the music is the thing that matters. I don't think its about what musicians think of any other musi-cians or what they might or might not think of each other. We were very lucky to be in a pop group, and we were very lucky to be in bands that had that effect on people it should for all of us, be a great honour that we made music that was the soundtrack to people's lives.

2-Tone@30

PAUL HESKETT-SWINGING CATS, AND FLUTE ON GHOST TOWN

How do I feel about the 30th anniversary of Two Tone? I wonder where all the intervening years have gone... I hope that there will be some really appropriate celebrations because it was an extraordinary movement which defined the lives of many of us, and I feel privileged and proud to have been associated with it.

What is remarkable is the continuing influence that the label has on pop music all these years later. So many contemporary bands and artists cite The Specials and the label as a major influence. The political landscape of our country has changed enormously since Jim Callaghan was Prime Minister and Margaret Thatcher took over; but many of the issues that were addressed in songs by bands like The Specials, The Selecter and The Beat remain, and new issues have entered our political consciousness, particularly the wars in Iraq and Afghanistan, globalisation, global warming and more immediately and most poignantly, the appalling rise in gun and knife crime. Which contemporary pop stars are addressing these issues in songs that make a difference?

I had some amazing experiences on the road with The Specials and my association with the band is still and always will be a source of enormous pride to me and to my children. Obviously to perform on Ghost Town which became an enduring cultural anthem and captured the zeitgeist was fantastic. If the original band had to have a swansong, then I am glad it was Ghost Town.

But I live in hope that a reunion will take place, as I write this in July 2008. If the collective will is strong enough, it may take place. Considerable obstacles remain, but I would like to keep a small amount of cautious optimism! I would love my children and a whole new generation of fans to experience that magic, which I believe we could collectively recreate.

NEOL DAVIES-SELECTER

My feelings about the 30th anniversary are simply that I'm pleased to be seeing it and pleased that it is something significant enough to warrant one...I am hugely proud of our achievement, not many other "things" have broken though from the street up to the level of 2Tone, where it continues to influence and have resonance globally: usually, in this country, there is the presence and assistance of old boy networks and show biz families that enable often 2nd rate artists to gain public awareness/success...that's how it works but it needs continual reminders to the London elite, for want of a better phrase but it'll do, that London bands are few and far between, most of the best culture originates "in the provinces".

51

2-Tone@30

HORACE PANTER-THE SPECIALS

To think that 30 years after we lugged our equipment up the two flights of stairs to Horizon Studios, (where the road leading to Coventry's Central 6 retail park is now), people would still be inspired by the music we made is ...er......inspiring. Nothing was organised for our 25th. anniversary, which is a more traditional type of anniversary, if you know what I mean, but there seems to be quite a groundswell of feeling around about the band at the moment, plus a 'Best Of' release.

The whole music business has changed drastically of late, with the age barrier being broken down. 20/30 years ago, no-one would be interested in anyone over 35, unless they were jazzers or bluesmen. Now , people flock to see The Rolling Stones, who's youngest member is 58 or something . Also, playing live is a big deal again, and if there was one thing The Specials were good at, it was playing live. I would like to think that our input into the 'world of pop' has been significant. Sonically, modern dance music sounds like reggae, and dub effects are prevalent across re-mixes and so on. I don't know whether people make songs that make you think and dance at the same time any more, but with the fracturing of genres and the multitude of ways of hearing contemporary music, it's difficult for me to find out. (This is a polite way of saying I'm out of touch!) My proudest memory of 2-Tone.....After a traditionally riotous gig in Portsmouth, I believe, Lynval was sitting on the lip of the stage talking with a young white kid who had the British Movement logo cut into his hair. The fact that our music could change negative into positive and that I helped to do that is something that no-one can take away from me.

ARTHUR 'GAPS' HENDRICKSON-THE SELECTER

It's nice that after thirty years it's still relevant, it's good to know that I was involved in something like this. My proudest moment is when it all came together and I think it was the first show that we played in London; I think it was the electric Ballroom. All the friends and family were there and Madness and everyone, it was a magical moment. It was also great to play with people like the Skatalites, because these guys were reggae originators and were my boyhood heroes and it was good to help bring music like theirs back into the limelight.

2-Tone@30

PAULINE BLACK-THE SELECTER

I am immensely proud that the music of the 2-Tone era seems to be just as relevant today in the current world-wide economic turndown, Middle East conflicts and street crime problems, as it was 30 years ago. Much of the music made at that time seems strangely prophetic when looked at in today's political climate. This is something that I consider the best testament to the continued relevance of songs like the Specials 'Ghost Town' , the Special A.K.A's 'War Crimes' or The Selecter's 'Too Much Pressure' and 'Celebrate The Bullet'. Also, the interest of an artist of the calibre of Amy Winehouse bears witness to 2-Tone's continuing relevance, especially since ska is traditionally a male dominated territory. The release of her limited edition spoof 2-tone E.P. underlines the fact that ska music has a far-reaching appeal when given a woman's touch.

My proudest memory of 2-Tone is being part of the first Two Tone Tour in 1979 was exciting. It was wonderful to feel part of a principled movement. These days, too many fans, both young and old forget that racism and sexism was rife at the time and I feel proud to have made a stand against those twin evils of society, at a period in time when a Thatcher government had just been elected. The 2 Tone bands had a reason for being, which went way beyond the usual pop band's remit of money and fame.

JAMES MACKIE-THE SELECTER

I'm not sure it can be 30 years because I'm only 29 years old and I know that a lot of the other guys are too. However, it is important to celebrate what I think is the last important musical movement this country has had. I was always on the outside of the movement a bit. I wasn't there from the start and only came in 1980 but I knew, then, how important it was - I was a fan first, then a player. Much of the music hasn't stopped being relevant and it's still the only thing that gets some blokes dancing! Best memories - front cover of Melody Maker, NEC, Whistle Test, watching Neol playing 'Celebrate the Bullet' on his Strat. - too many to mention".

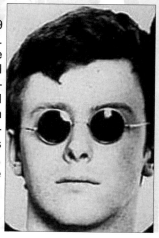

A Special Road to Reunion

It's been a rocky road, but by the time you read this book, you will know that That six former Specials have reformed and played their first concert at The Bestival the Isle of Wight, September 2008. Anyone who thinks this reunion has been easy to make happen is fooling themselves. For this was the mother of all square pegs in round holes, but the guys pulled it off, with a lot of input from Lynval Golding and project manager Steve Blackwell of course.

Wherever I go, people keep asking me, "When are the Specials getting back together?" How do I know, OK I get to hear things from various camps. I thought it was about time to put it down in writing. So In November 2007 I wrote a Backbeat in the Coventry Telegraph. Should the Specials get back together, or not? It was a sit on the fence type thing. Though the 'for reforming' copy was a lot bigger than the against copy. Features Editor John West, suggested I equalled them up a little, ooopps, don't want to look too keen. In mid November I get a call from Lynval Golding, "Special Brew are playing tonight at the Jaguar club and Horace and Roddy are to guests. Be great to see you for a chat". "I was planning on going anyway, so I'll see you there, I replied".

I find Lynval and we begin to chat. We talk about my "should the Specials reform Backbeat article". "That's kind of what I want to talk to you about", said Lynval. I don't recall the conversation word for word, but the gist is that all seven Specials met about four weeks ago. The first time they had all been in the same room in many years. I broke out in a huge grin, just like the one Lynval was wearing. "Basically we all want this", Lynval revealed, "We may not yet be all singing from the same hymn sheet", but one way or another we are getting back together next year to play". I nearly cried. At this point Horace and Roddy came over; Lynval had already told them that he was going to let me in on this. It was great to see smiles all round; yes they really did want this! The three of them got on stage and vocalist Simon Kelly said, "make the most of three Specials on stage together, cus you will never see it again". Maybe not, I thought to myself. I was literally grinning like a Cheshire cat, my wife had to tell me to tone it down.

The set that night was superb, and for those who knew, saw it as a taster of what would come. Even Lynval finished his set with "See you next year". People began asking, what did he mean by that? So because I had happened to write a pretty throw away article, I had discovered what was to come, although at the time I had no idea it would take the best part of a year to materialise with so much going on in between. I had originally intended to include an Onion Blog in these pages, most people who read it felt that the ins and outs of the mechanics of bringing the band back were boring and I simply hadn't addressed some of the more delicate matters (not my style I'm happy to say). So I'll leave the warts 'n' all story to someone far better qualified to do it. So here's my Onion Blog lite version.

Hoz, Rodd and Lynval on stage with Special Brew, November 2007.

Specials fans will know that the rumours grew and grew, late November 2007 the word was that the guys had rehearsed together and some dates were coming up, of course this didn't occur. There was some good news in December concerning the pending release of a Specials DVD released in February 2008 "Too Much Too Young" (basically the video hits on DVD). In January the reunion looks to be on, but with how many original members?

Late January the BBC Midlands Today news, ran a piece about Horace Panter, and his work as a Special Needs teacher. There was Horace in his black and white check apron, in the classroom with his pupils. A lovely piece that showed a classroom full of mementoes of those heady days, what was of interest here to the blog was the biggest Onion hint so far. When Horace was asked if the Specials would ever reunite he replied. "Watch this space, something may very well work out later this year". Oh you little tease Mr. Panter. The next we hear was talk of May gigs, then the talk of legalities and all that stuff, and the rumour that the Specials would be on the cover of Mojo magazine! Then come the end of February, the reunion looked doomed, and all seemed lost. The lads are to embark on a round of interviews for the pending Best of Specials CD/DVD release, no doubt they will be asked the reunion question during these interviews? Hang on a minute though, the word on the street is the reunion looks on again, planned for October no less.

So the news is that the Specials (or at least some of them), are to do a string of interviews to plug the 'Best of' package. Obviously it's something that had to be covered in my Backbeat column. One question that they would be asked probably by every interviewer is about a reunion! So hey I too had to pose the question too (be impolite not to). Both Horace and Lynval, were more than happy to answer my questions, including that rather tricky one. They were totally honest and said it how it was, and they virtually said it would happen. Horace said of the reunion, "We are currently talking (to one another) about the possibilities of performing some concerts in October, but three months ago we were talking about doing some concerts in May - and that didn't happen. Personally I'm optimistic; a few people are making noises about 30th anniversary, blah blah blah". While Lynval said, "I can see no reason why not; it's been a slow process. It's taken me five years to get to this stage, all seven of us did actually get together last year, and four of us have rehearsed together (Lynval, Brad, Roddy and Horace). I hope it isn't going to take another five years before we actually perform. It's something that will have to happen. I've worked very hard to make this happen, I have done all I can do".

Lynval kindly also said about me, "On that point I would really, really like to thank you (Pete Chambers) from the bottom of my heart. The one man out of everyone, who kept this whole thing moving over the years has been you. It's not just me alone it was you as well who has helped make this happen and kept it alive".

One guy on the website had this to say about my interview. "Well ... I have just come home tonight to see a full page article devoted to the Specials, in the Coventry Telegraph - under the Pete Chambers 'Nostalgia' section. What a great article and very interesting read. As Lynval points out 'Pete' has done the Specials proud and kept the 2-tone engine running for the last few years. What was interesting was that the re-union tour is a real possibility both from Horace and Lynval's perspective. However, the greatest revelation was the fact 'all' 7 met up last year and four of them have been rehearsing together".

A voice comes on my phone, "Ello Pete its Nev". He's confirming that he will be at the unveiling of the Specials Walk of Fame star on 16th May. Also letting me know that he's supporting The Enemy at The Ricoh next Sunday. I get asked to participate in a Central TV piece, claiming in the headlines that the Specials are to reform. It turned out to be for a rehearsal rather than the 'real' thing. Neville did a piece for Central news, saying the reunion may happen.

Late March and rehearsals have taken place with all Specials in attendance (though not all at the same time due to transport problems) and Lynval is overjoyed, It was bloody brilliant he says. We played Stereotype" said Lyn, "and we were all just smiling at each other it sounded so good, none of us wanted to stop" Horace too is happy with things, Rod & I travelled for nine and a half hours to play just over one hour of music, but it was pretty incredible music. I am still speechless. Horace. In April I meet up with Neville Staple, we are both doing interviews for local BBC TV about the Enemy gigs at the Ricoh over the weekend. According to Nev, "They need time to rehearse, we need to get it right, if we are to do it"

Two days later and Neville plays the 2nd Enemy gig at the 8,000 capacity Jaguar Hall, in the Ricoh complex. Nev and his band are spot on. A great weekend all round, until rumours that the reunion was off again, and it turns out to be true. I turn on my TV and the BBC announce that the Specials are to reform!! Nice timing lads.

Many of the Radio interviews to plug 'The Best Of' package took place at the BBC Coventry & Warwickshire, including one very interesting one with Bob Brolly.

May 16th is Walk of Fame day, Jerry send this great message, "I just want to say that I really appreciate The Specials being recognised in this way, and want to thank all the people who voted for the band". Jerry Dammers (founder Specials and 2 Tone). I catch up with Horace and Roddy, who despite not knowing what to expect of the day seemed to enjoy it. By June there had been more rehearsals, still no real news, it may be next year now we hear. The positive news is the Specials are to receive a Mojo Award. Can I offer huge congratulations to The Spe-

cials for being inducted into the exclusive Mojo Hall of Fame. They join other music luminary's like The Doors, Madness and Elton John. After nearly thirty years the band and their music are still relevant. Five of the band members were present, (Neville Staple was on tour in Ireland and didn't make it).I spoke to a very excited Lynval Golding who was amazed at the amount of people asking them when they are you guys getting back together. "Even Phil Collins asked me, Lynval said. "It was an amazing night, to sit with Neil Diamond, and I met my guitar hero Jimmy Page. This night really sums up why we really should be playing as the Specials again"!

The Boys receive their award, thanks to Alex Ogg for the photo.

20th June, It's Nelson Mandela's 90th Birthday celebration concert in London, Jerry Dammers, who of course wrote 'Free Nelson Mandela'. Leads a star-studded chorus that includes Amy Winehouse on lead vocals, and members of Queen. Godiva Festival arrives, it's raining, and The Enemy are topping the bill, yet everyone is talking about The Specials and 2-Tone! Early July I meet up with Lynval at Browns in Coventry. He dictates his foreword for this book to me over breakfast. I take him to Priory Place and show him the Walk of Fame, and the Specials star. He's well impressed and dedicates it to his late Father, we go to the BBC and meet up with presenter Bob Brolly, who like on many occasions, wants to know when they are all getting back together? Everywhere I go, it's Specials, Specials, Selecter, 2-Tone and Specials. Wow, do these guys really understand what they have done for this city, and the world of popular music?

Just as reunion hopes fall to an all time low, the latest news is something may be happening in September. Loads of rehearsals are taking place, and a brass section called in. The name Bestival has been mentioned, then confirmed, they intend to make their comeback on 6th September 2008, at the Isle of Wight Bestival. Apparently they are the 'Mystery Band', as the name the Specials and Special AKA is still part of a legal wrangle.

An exclusive rehearsal shot, photo copyright of Pete Chambers

A Special Night In Glorious Black & Wight.

We thought it may never happen, indeed a year ago it looks distinctly unlikely, but on Saturday 6th September, 2008, six of the original Specials (Terry Hall, Horace Panter, Lynval Golding, John Bradbury, Roddy Byers and Nev Staple) played together for the first time in twenty-seven years at the Isle of Wight's Bestival, and I'm so pleased to say I was there!

Anyone who thinks that getting to this situation has been easy should think again. I was first let in on the 'secret' in November last year, since then it's been a rollercoaster ride, of would they or wouldn't they, and if so how many? One day good, next day bad. So feelings on Saturday were born more out of sheer relief than just plain excitement. Even now there are complications, with the six unable to use the Specials (or Special AKA) names, now owned by the only original member not to be part of the reunion, Jerry Dammers.

Before we get to the gig, let me rewind a little to the previous Wednesday. I was granted exclusive access to a "Special" last production Rehearsal, somewhere in Warwickshire (actually the superb Assembly rooms in Leamington). Excited? Just a little, not only were the boys back, but I was going to see the full show tonight. All my Birthdays and Christmases were about to come in one go. It was all very clandestine; mercifully I wasn't blindfolded for the journey. So much so I was only one of four guests in attendance (excluding family and crew of course) and proud to be the only journalist to be given this mega-exclusive preview! When Horace and myself arrived Roddy was already there, we were closely followed by Terry, Brad, Lynval and finally Neville. After what seemed like hours of sound checks, the band assembled on stage, it was shivers down the spine time as the six took their position on the stage. From Left to right, Roddy, Horace, Neville, Brad, Terry,Lynval and the new keyboard player Nikolij. Nev approached the mike, and Coventry's finest were back together, doing what they do best, playing iconic ska music. This was about their twelfth rehearsal, but the first one where all of the members were present at the same time, and this was the full show.

Backbeat readers are probably expecting me to get carried away here, but it really did sound amazing! All the main elements were present, like Brad's distinct drum style, Horace's imaginative bass lines, Terry and Nev's voices were spot on, stronger than ever. While Rodd and Lynval were nailing with their respective guitar parts. I kept looking away, then looking back at the stage, to reassure myself, yep, it's real alright, they are there and they are making great music again. Nite Klub was musically outstanding, and probably the best I have ever heard it!

Lynval reveals that, "It amazing being back, it's like it's the 1980-something again, it just feels no natural. It's all back, the sound, the vibe the connection between each person and instrument. It feels like a little gang again, and our unity is the glue that holds it all together. Instrumentally there is just a great improvement, you can really hear it." I asked Lynval how it feels that it will actually happen. "Well Pete, you and me have been struggling for five years, we have been keeping at this, and it's finally come true that we are doing our first gig. I would have loved it to have been Coventry but I will be working to get the band to come and do the Coventry Godiva Festival next year. I've got nine months to twist everyone's arm, so my aim is we will be back in Coventry playing Godiva".

The festival was the usual fare of mud, wellies, good humour, rain, wristbands and more mud. The Special Guests took to the stage at 5.15 just as the heavens opened again. That had no effect of the assembled 2-Tone fans who had been let in on the secret, and none of them could quite believe what was about to happen! The strains of Jerusalem began playing, and the voice (that of actor Nick Moran) reminded us that the issues of 30 years ago were still relevant today and so was this band. At this we hear Neville's dulcet tones, "Bernie Rhodes knows Don't Argue", and Gangsters gets this huge slice of history on the way. Without getting carried away, it was a near-perfect set, they sounded amazing, and they looked so sharp. The crowd still loved them and everyone seemed to know the songs.

It was a monumental gig, and testament to all the work that has been put in, to make this happen, especially from the likes of Lynval Golding and manager Steve Blackwell. After the show, I spoke to celebrity fan Simon Jordan who had been singing along to every song side stage, I asked what he thought he replied something like "bloomin' marvellous", and Comedian and Ska fan Phill Jupitus, declared, It's like I went to sleep in 1979, and I've suddenly woken up again", I heard that this may happen about four months ago, and now it has It's just incredible". Indeed, the whole band were simply glowing backstage, Lynval who was a big mover in making this happen was loving every moment of it and wanted to do it again right away, right now with a full set. It was an emotional day, espe-

Ska's finest backstage with Lynval

cially when it all began to sink in. I had dreamed of this for so long, and now the secret was out and I can declare that the boys are back, and don't argue!

Here's the full set list, Gangsters, (Dawning of A) New Era, Do the Dog, It's Up To You, Monkey Man, Rat Race, A Message To You Rudy, Nite Klub, Little Bitch, Too much Too Young, Blank Expression, Concrete Jungle (Roddy on vocals), Too Hot, It Doesn't make It Alright and You're Wondering Now.

A Very Special Guitar

Coventry Market has most generously donated a Fender Telecaster guitar as a raffle prize as part of the Markets promotion of this very book. So I took the opportunity on the night of rehearsal to get it signed by all of the guys.

Exclusive rehearsal shots, photo copyright of Pete Chambers

THE DAWNING OF A NEW ERA– The Rude Boys at Bestival 2008

THE DAWNING OF A NEW ERA– The Rude Boys at Bestival 2008

Above Lynval and Simon Jordan.
Below Lyn, Phill Jupitus and Nikolij

THE DAWNING OF A NEW ERA– The Rude Boys at Bestival 2008

Walt's back in town!

All Bestival photos by Pete Chambers

THE DAWNING OF A NEW ERA– The Rude Boys at Bestival 2008

THE DAWNING OF A NEW ERA– The Rude Boys at Bestival 2008

The Specials   the pride of Coventry

The Revised 30th Anniversary version

2-Tone Trail
by Pete Chambers

The definitive guide to Two Tone Coventry

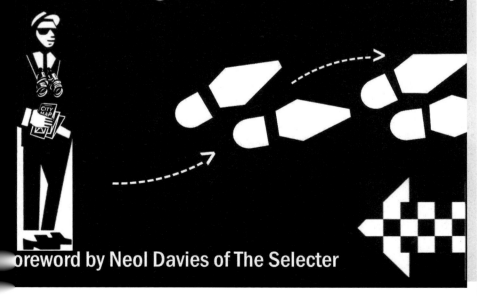

Foreword by Neol Davies of The Selecter

Forward By Neol Davies

Reflecting on the history of 2-Tone there seems to be a sense of "it could only have happened here." Coventry is known internationally as a place of Peace and Reconciliation. This message, with the fresh 2-Tone style of live music and dancing was energetically communicated to the world by The Specials and The Selecter in 1979, albeit in a context of personal and racial tolerance rather than its more usual wartime references.

The City constantly changes while stubbornly retaining its attitude and vibe, which has meant that many 2-Tone locations, have been lost. Perhaps the most important of these places was Horizon Studios, a former railway stable block and warehouse. It was here "Gangsters" was recorded and "The Selecter" was re-mixed to create "Gangsters Vs. The Selecter", the first 2-Tone single. Regrettably, it's photos only for Horizon Studios but there are plenty of interesting places to visit and discover on the 2-Tone Trail, thanks to this long over-due book.

What was really special about 2-Tone, aside from the great music, was the attempt to change things and maybe people's thinking with an inclusive - almost co-operative - approach. Bands working together instead of entirely out for themselves. We knew we were working against the grain but that only seemed to make us more determined. Something about this city's character informed all of the band members' attitudes and after years of forming different bands and trying to create original music, we were all fortunate to be there to make it happen.

The deep and lasting effect we had on so many people all over the world has made me feel proud of 2-Tone's achievements, and the next generations of talented musicians and singers have pursued many re-interpretations of The Ska that inspired us.

Now, for the first, time all of the locations that are historically important to the 2Tone Story have been mapped out in this book. As you roam the City to visit these places I hope you experience some of the resonances that helped to form the mindset of The Specials and The Selecter at the end of the 1970's.

It's difficult to argue that Coventry is a fabulous metropolitan icon of culture and good taste but... there's nowhere like it anywhere. It's good to be unique.

Neol

Spring 2005

Updated

ack in 2005, I wrote what was to be my second book, The 2-Tone Trail. Basically a tour of oventry's Specials and Selecter sites. It proved to be a massive success, and sold all ver the world. Sadly (or gladly), the book sold out, and rarely does a week go by without omeone requesting to buy a copy. So here is an update 30th Anniversary style.

The Places and Faces in 2-Tone Coventry

Velcome to The 2 Tone Trail Guide of Coventry, "your host town not a ghost town"! This uide is designed to give the music/2 Tone/Specials/Selecter fan a little personal insight ito where the 2-Tone phenomenon began. For so long a hint of 2-Tone in Coventry has een an illusive affair. With this book I hope to give tourists and locals alike something angible to connect with in this black & white melting pot we call Cov'. So while you're on ie trail, stand back and stop for a while, drink in the atmosphere. Try to imagine how it 'as, when local boy and muso' genius Jerry Dammers along with Neol Davies and the ther top players of 2-Tone finally saw it all coming to fruition. Many would say it only isted a couple of years, well yes maybe it did, but they were two of the most exciting fun-acked years you could imagine. I'm just happy to have been around at the time.

i this book each site entry is designed to give as much information you need without be-oming too long-winded. You will also read quotes from various members of the 2-Tone oster. These are all new and exclusive to this book. I would like to thank Jerry Dammers, lorace Panter, Roddy Byers and Neol Davies for checking the information in this publica-on for any inaccuracies.

he book can be used as a stand-alone reference guide, but if you fancy doing the actual -Tone trail of Coventry. just a few things to bear in mind though! The core trail takes in nainly Coventry City Centre this includes all the 'real' pertinent 2-Tone sites tracked out as iethodically as possible . It should take around 2 hours. So sensible footwear is advised e recommend loafers, Royal's or for extra comfort Dr Martens (14 eyelet recommended).

he out of town sites lie in the city suburbs (obviously), so transport of some kind is ad-ised, also some of the sites are residential/private and are on busy roads. So beware of affic and please respect the privacy of residents at the locations.

njoy yourself!

ete Chambers, spring 2005

The revised start point of the trail is now located outside of the BBC Coventry & Warwickshire Radio Station, in Priory Place. If you locate the huge Whittle Arches structure, (opposite the Transport Museum) you will find the BBC and The Walk of Fame like a pot of gold at the end of a metal rainbow.

(S) Star and Start Point, (Priory Place) At last Coventry has something tangible to show Specials fans. I'm proud to have initiated the project, mainly to see some sort of 2-Tone tribute in the city.

Crossing Priory Place diagonally are the first ten stars (more will follow). Of immediate interest to 2-Tone fans, will be The Specials star and a star dedicated to the bands first real manager Pete Waterman. The plaques were unveiled on 16th May 2008. In attendance for the Specials was Horace and Roddy.

THE SPECIALS
2-TONE BAND

Above The Specials WOF star (and close-up), right Roddy and Horace decide who gets the award, and above Hoz and the former manager Pete Waterman OBE.

Lynval seemed well impressed with the star judging by the way he knelt down at the plaque. When asked how he felt about this award he replied, 'I would like to dedicate it to my Father who is now at rest in Holbrook's Cemetery, I'm sure he would be very proud of what his son has Achieved".

Directions from the Walk of Fame, in Priory Place, head for the top corner by the water feature you will see the Priory Undercroft. Continue past this, over the small road ,ignoring the hotel. Continue forward, the vista should be dominated by Priory Hall in front of you. You will come out by Coventry Cathedral's Chapel of Unity, turn right and just before the Cathedral steps, cross over into University Square. The Lanch entrance steps are across the square over to your left.

(1) The Lanchester Polytechnic, (Priory Street) In the Specials days it
was known as "The Lanch", the Main Hall in the Student Union building was where most of the action took place. In the 70's you could have expected to see the likes of Thin Lizzy, Caravan, ELO, ELP, Stone the Crows (the support was provided by Mead who included Neol Davies in their ranks). It remained a place of 'rock' for many years. The Specials played here (supported by The Swinging Cats) in September 1980, it was a great gig and even Suggs from Madness was in attendance.

The Lanch was the chosen venue for Covaid, Coventry's answer to Live Aid took place on October 19th 1985. Two Tone related people on the bill were Pauline Black in The Supernaturals and headlining were Colourfield including of course Terry Hall from The Specials and Toby Lyons from The Swinging Cats and Jerry was the DJ that day. The

Specials filmed the video for the single Rat Race in the main hall. They also signed their Chrysalis contract in the Uni' bar. The idea for the song was also conceived at the Lanch's upstairs bar when, Roddy Radiation overheard some well-to-do students discussing jobs that their parents had lined up for them on leaving college! For the video each member of the group took on the persona of an archetypal teacher. Roddy Byers recalls that video shoot "I remember Lynval and Neville arguing about who was going to be the gym Teacher, Lynval won that one of course. The kids were pretending to do exams in the video, and I can tell you they were writing down some funny and interesting things". Apparently Jerry Dammer's portrayal of a wicked school matriarch was so convincing the video was banned so all the nice boys and girls could sleep soundly in their beds. Many years later Horace would become a teacher for real. The 'exam' scene has been recreated at least twice for the TV cameras, including a feature for the 2-Tone Trail for ITV, invoking memories from Nev and Roddy.

Neville in the Lanch Main Hall referencing the 2-Tone Trail 2005 part of a Central TV shoot.

Neville recalled how someone stole one of Horaces's Bass guitars, from the main Hall during a show. It was literally smuggled through the back window. Apparently Nev met the guy who stole it some years later, no sign of the 4 string though!

Other 2-Tone people who attended the Poly were Pauline Black who studied Bio-chemistry and Horace Panter and Jerry Dammers who got their art degrees here (but Jerry never bothered to pick his up).

The Lanch circa 1979

Jerry Dammers-"I wasn't exactly your normal art student, after my foundation year at Nottingham my first choice of college was Leeds. I didn't take any paintings to the interview. I tried to pull a "Pete Townsend" type scam, I told them I was going to create a "pop art" band instead of doing any paintings! I said it would be like "a modern version of the Who" all I had was a tape of me singing "Little Bitch" (which the Specials ended up doing about 4 years later). The professor doing the interview just laughed and shook his head in disbelief and showed me the door! I had to come back to my second choice of college, Coventry, where I showed them my paintings and got in. If it hadn't been for that bold and crazy move at the first interview I might have actually got in at Leeds college and there would have been no Specials and no 2 -Tone as we know it "!

Jerry did make a return to Coventry University in November 2005, and was awarded with an Honorary Degree. The ceremony as always, carried out in Coventry Cathedral, with tea and biscuits (and photographs) in the University it's self.

The Boys at the Lanch, rude boys wear plaid.

2-TONE PRESENTS

THE SPECIALS

and

SWINGING CATS

IN CONCERT AT

COVENTRY (LANCHESTER) POLYTECHNIC STUDENTS UNION

THURSDAY, 25th SEPTEMBER

and

FRIDAY, 26th SEPTEMBER

8 p.m.

TICKETS £3 from The Students Union and Virgin Records, Coventry

Graphic Press (Coventry) Ltd., 111 Harnall Lane East, Coventry

Top, The Specials at The Lanch in 1980 and Jerry DJ's at Covaid. Left, The Lanch as seen in the Rat Race video. Below Left: Backstage at the Lanch Below Right: Suggs at the Poly bar.

From The Lanch continue across the square heading towards the glass entrance of the new Herbert Gallery & Museum. Turn left walk past front of Herbert, cross road at zebra crossing The Ellen Terry Building is further on the right. (The Herbert has a good 2-Tone archive collection.)

(2) The Odeon Cinema (Jordan Well) I saw many films here including Dance

Craze on 3rd March 1981. A well used promotion photo of The Specials was taken on the roof of this building (, now fittingly The Ellen Terry Building, a faculty for the performing arts and communications. "The shoot was done during a long day's photographing around Cov City centre, reveals Horace Panter." Other locations included the old Odeon theatre, on the roof - quite scary; don't look down sort of vibe. Brad was suffering from a migraine of Richter-scale proportions, which explains the somewhat pained expression he wears in most of the photos. We used one of the shots for the back of the 2nd Album too, I really have come to hate those white brogue shoes I wore".

From the Odeon building proceed across Whitefriars Rd to Phoenix pub, the Oak is next door.

(3) The Oak Inn (Gosford Street) A

central contact point in the formative years fo Jerry, Brad and Neol, Neol remembers tha the floor was black and white check. It was after a night in here that Jerry came up with the name The Specials.

The Oak Inn, right circa 1979 and above the boys on the Odeon roof. Picture left by Chalkie Davies & Carol Starr

Right, The Specials on the Odeon's roof.

Below, The Odeon in 1980 not showing Dance Craze we presume, and main picture, front of house with the Odeon's manageresses.

Carry straight on under flyover away from City centre for half a mile to Far Gosford Street.

(4) Far Gosford Street

A street that always seemed to be rather neglected , it did however contain a plethora of second hand (thrift) shops that kept our 2 Tone warriors in tonic jackets ('please let it have a ticket pocket') and as much collectable vinyl as their Dancettes could cope with. Horace Panter once had a flat in Bramble Street just off Gosford St (No 70). Sites in the area were Ramp Studios where the reformed Specials demoed tracks for Today's Specials (upstairs at 139). Hits Misses and Vintage Records was the Mecca for Cov' record collectors (now a restaurant), Phil Oakey's brother Bob once owned a music shop in the street. Indeed nowadays all the City's musical instrument shops are centred around this area, as is Backbeat rehearsal Studios and Noise Works guitar shop. "There was talk of buying the old Paris cinema in Gosford Street to convert into a 2-Tone H.Q./studio/club in 1980, it's now The Riley's pool hall"- Horace Panter. The public house, The Cup (now The Beer Engine) was the site of Selecter rehearsals, Roddy's Tearjerkers have also played here. The Hand and Heart pub was an early venue for The Selecter and The Specials also played the venue a few times and as part of their Lightening Tour of Coventry in 1978.

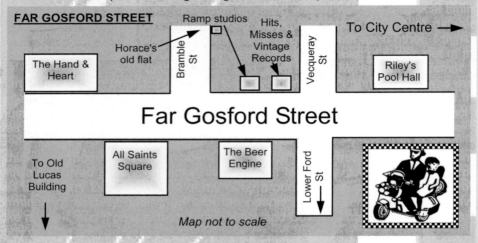

Map not to scale

Cut through All Saints Square (you will see a steel archway) and cross road at crossing, follow path round to Access building that was once Lucas Aerospace.

(5) Lucas Aerospace Building

(Read Street). Now an Access storage warehouse but once the place Neol Davies of The Selecter called work. He tells of one occasion when all was going wrong, he had argued with his wife, his car had failed the MOT and as he went back to work after lunch he turned to a female colleague and declared he had 'Too much pressure' within a few minutes a great song (and album title) was born.

Top left The Beer Engine, top right the reformed Specials in Ramp studios. Middle left The Mk2 Specials in Gosford St. Middle right The Hand & Heart and bottom The former Lucas building.

Specials Photos courtesy ITV Central News.

Neville and fans outside the Beer Engine, and right Hits, Misses & Vintage Records.

Continue to follow the path round, down East Street, you will eventually come to The Binley Oak public house.

(6) The Binley Oak Public House (Britannia Street) It was here that

The Specials got their 'ska' thing together, though they would never actually play here live. You're Wondering Now was learnt at the Binley Oak (once the scene of the influential Motown House) One rehearsal was less than happy for Silverton and he quit the band and Drummer John Bradbury was quickly drafted in. Horace came back here for the Ghost Town documentary and he and Lynval returned here in 2007, to promote Horace's book on local TV. Pauline Black also successfully auditioned for the Selecter here or was it an audition. This is what Pauline had to say on the matter. "I turned up for rehearsal (if I was auditioning, then I wasn't aware of it!), it transpired that I had written a song that we could work on 'They Make Me Mad', which ended up on the first album 'Too Much Pressure', along with another of my compositions 'Black and Blue'. Nobody ever said 'hey you're in', I just carried on singing with them. I don't really think that they knew what to make of me. I didn't fit the mould of the usual 'black girl singer' and I had very definite political views, but I could write songs too, which nobody other than Neol seemed to be able to do at that time".

The Binley Oak inside and out!

Continue straight on for about one mile, through the area of Hillfields. On the way you will come to a small shopping precinct on the right, this is the Village Square, scene of the Selecter's first NME photo shoot. Moving on you will come to Sidney Stringer on the left and The Kasbah right.

(7) Sidney Stringer Comprehensive School (Cox Street) Terry

Hall went to school here. The school is located in Hillfields (as name checked in the song Fearful composed by Horace Panter from the 1998 album Guilty 'Til Proved Innocent!).) An area that was home to many of the musicians that would become The Selecter. It was here Neol Davies first met and rehearsed with Hardtop 22 who would form the core of The Selecter. Selecter's Gaps Hendrickson recalls the day Neol Davies turned up at the school guitar in hand. "Charley had disappeared for a couple of days and came back and told us we had a meeting. He never explained it was with Neol, (who most of us knew at that point). So when Neol turned up explaining to us what his plans were and how he saw things musically, we all began wondering why he was telling us this. Eventually it was made plain of course that we would become The Selecter, that had up until that point remained just a Specials B-Side". The school suffered extensive fire damage in 2007.

Right, Sidney Stringer School, before the fire.

Left, The Selecter live at The Tic Toc.

(8)The Tic Toc Club (Primrose Hill Street) A building with a long musical his-

tory, became the Orchid Ballroom in the early sixties. The night club was managed by Larry Page-who managed the Kinks-who included Ray Davies-who had a child with Chrissie Hynde-who did backing vocals on The Specials song Nite Club (the circle is complete). It later became The Tic-Toc Club, with more than a little help from Jon Gaunt (now a wellknows shock jock and TV star) in 1991 it faced closure and a group of 2-Tone people played as part of a benefit evening. The Special Beat also played The Tic Toc (and recorded a live album here), apparently going down as one of the venues best gigs. It also hosted another conglomerate 2-tone band in the shape of The International Beat. A reformed Selecter played the venue many times, even hiring it for tour rehearsals and recorded the live album Out On The Streets Again here on December 21st 1991. Jerry Dammers had a short DJ residency here in the 90's. It continued to be a house of musical fun as The Colosseum, where on February 9th 2007, The Enemy played A Message To You Rudy and Too Much Too Young, with guest star Neville Staples. The venue has since been reinvented as the Kasbah.

Top right, the
Selecter in the
Village Square
Hillfields .
Photo by Chris
Horler.

Middle: Left Roger,
Jerry, Neol, Aitch,
Lynval and Roddy
outside the Tic Toc.

Middle Right Jerry
and Co play the Tic
Toc

Bottom: Left and
Right posters for the
Tic Toc

Taking Blue Beat and Ska into
the 90's.....

SPECIAL bEAT

with Rankin' Roger. Neville Staples
and many more

RECENTLY TAKEN THE U.S. BY STORM

SATURDAY 4TH MAY

Tickets £6.00 adv. Doors 8pm

TIC TOC   Primrose Hill Street
Coventry

SPECIAL bEAT

2 TONE   2 TONE   2 TONE

The
International

bEAT

2 TONE   2 TONE

+ Support 8 - 2pm £5 adv
Saturday 11th January

Box Office 0203 630877
PRIMROSE HILL STREET COVENTRY

TICKETS ALSO AVAILABLE FROM
Coventry - Poster Place Soundhouse, Spin-a-Disc, Rage,
Birmingham - Tempest Records, HMV Swanston
Kenilworth & Warwick - Discotrak,
Leamington Spa - Music Junction,
Rugby - Discovery Records,
Stratford upon Avon - No Pep No Style.

Continue straight ahead under flyover, turn immediately right. Walk through medieval arch (Cook St Gate), follow road around to large building with fire escapes. This is the Ko Poda nightclub, formerly the City Centre Club.

(9) The City Centre Club (now Demand, Tower Street). Really just a

nightclub (Nite Klub, is this the in place to be Nite club, what am I doing here Nite club, watching the girls go by spending money on...)(lyrics courtesy of Plangent Vision music Ltd) The Specials and The Selecter played here on 31st July 1979. I remember queuing outside when one of the bouncers had refused Roddy Radiation admission. That was until the whole queue informed the doorman that there would be no concert if he wasn't allowed in! In the hilarious Specials Illustrated Songbook by Nick Davies, Nick illustrates a membership card for the 'City Centre Fite Spot'!

Above, Inside the City Centre Club.

Left, the club in it's Pink Parrott period

From Ko Poda, continue past Royal Mail building (as seen on the rear of the More Specials album). As you enter the street turn right and you will see the bridge to the Canal Basin. The Canal Basin by the way is a good place for refreshments and toilet stop, we can recommend The Country Crust Tea-Rooms for both.

(10) Canal Basin

It was here the front & back covers of The Specials first album and the rear cover of their second album *More Specials* were shot. The canal basin today is a lot more pleasant than the run-down area we saw on the rear of *More Specials.* It's a real canal again and the locale has shops and flats thanks to a huge shot of TLC. Jerry Dammers had thought about basing a 2 Tone HQ here, but like the Paris Cinema idea, it never happened.

The photographers that day were Chalkie Davies and Carol Starr Now running a successful photographic business in the US, I asked Chalkie about that day in Coventry. "Jerry had a couple of ideas for the sleeve photography, he liked the photo on the Who album My Generation with the four guys looking up. So we went to the canal basin, I recall there were a bunch of prison inmates cleaning it up that day. The front and back of the first album are the same picture from two different view points. One picture is taken from the first floor of a building looking down. Then a picture in exactly the same place taken from the side. We did some pictures on the boat, the canal didn't have any water in it I remember.

We played around with the cover, the Americans got the back picture on the front cover. We tried to make it look like a 60's sleeve. We took the Chrysalis butterfly logo off the sleeve cus' it sucked, then someone called me and said the Specials had two choices. They can either not have a record label or they can put the butterfly back on!" (It would seem that the Specials got their way in the end, cus' checking out Jason & Peter's very excellent site "2-Tone.Info", it seems that only the Australian version had the butterfly logo on it!) Chalkie again, "We then went to the roof of the cinema (see

location 2). It was a Saturday so we had to get finished by 4.40 so we didn't get chased by football hooligans". "I never thought it was going to be as big as it was, Neville Staple admitted. "We were just having some photo's taken, simple as that, I never dreamed how iconic those covers would turn out, even going on to be caricatured in Nick Davies's book . All I can remember of the day is the guys saying "look up here", as they took the photos". Lynval meanwhile had this to say on the event. "My memories of shooting the album cover was everybody in a miserable mood, looking up and waiting for something to happen".

Above left, the first Specials album rear cover and right a 2005 pastiche with Horace and Roddy also taken at the Canal basin. Below another view of the Coventry Canal Basin circa 1979 and more Chalkie Davies & Carol Starr photography. *Album cover shots are the copyright of EMI Publishing Limited, and are used with thanks.*

These following shots are all rare never before seen Canal Basin shots from Chalkie Davies and Carol Starr. I am indebted to Paul 'Willo' Williams, for his kindness in letting me use these photos he has obtained from Chalkie & Carol. I'm also indebted to Chalkie & Carol for their kindness it letting me use their photographs. As Chalkie said, "the Specials were Special".

Photo by Chalkie Davies and Carol Starr

SPECIALS

▚▚▚ SPECIALS

Photo by Chalkie Davies and Carol Starr

Photo by Chalkie Davies and Carol Starr

Top another Chalkie & Carol canal basin photo, middle left the rear cover art of the More Specials LP. Bottom left Horace & Roddy at the Canal basin May 2005. . Bottom, Nev and Roddy do the 2-Tone Trail for Central TV in October 2005.

Retrace steps over bridge, carry straight towards traffic lights, Parsons Nose is on the Right.

(11) The Parson's Nose Chip Shop (Bishop St). A fave' with the

club set and local band set in the city, There is a well known picture of The Specials outside the shop indulging in a french fry feeding frenzy, or as Terry Hall puts it in the song Friday Night Saturday Morning. "But 2 O Clock has come again It's time to leave this paradise, hope the chip shop isn't closed' Cause their pies are really nice". It ceased trading in 2003. The building now faces demolition, despite being just a one-off photo location, the Parsons, has featured on at least three Specials TV features.

Above and left Not Pearl's Café, but The Parson's Nose hope the chips weren't 'Too Hot', right The Holyhead Youth Club entrance.

From The Parsons Nose turn right into main road by traffic lights. Continue along Corporation Street past The Coventry Telegraph Offices (who have written a lot about 2-Tone of course) and The Belgrade Theatre (this was the venue for the 2-Tone influenced stage show Three Minute Hero). Continue on past St John's Church, turn right into Lower Holyhead Road (close by is the bar Tin Angel, the room above was the HQ for Shack Records) and half way down on the right to come to the Artspace, the Building that was once The Holyhead Youth Club. The basement's entrance is on the right of the building.

12) The Holyhead Youth Club (Lower Holyhead Road) Just a base-

ment in the mid 70's, but defining moment in 2-Tone history. It was here that blues influenced reggae was mixed by the likes of Neol Davies, Ray King, Lynval Golding and Silverton. "It was here where I first met Jerry", Neville reveals, "I had a sound system, it was set up there all the time, Jerry, Lynval, Horace and Tim Strickland used to rehearse downstairs". Selecter-to-be Charley Anderson had been a voluntary youth worker here with Coventry City Council. The place received grants from Cadbury's Trust for renovation. It was also here that the need for a purpose built youth based recording studio came into the mind of Amos Anderson, the idea later became The Glasshouse.

Continue to end of the road. Turn left and follow path to the side of the ring road. You will come to the Sky Dome on the left, in front is the subway (underpass). Turn right to end of tunnel, then left through next tunnel at exit take ramp. Quarter of a mile in front (look for floodlights) is the new Butts Stadium the college is next door.

(13) The Butts Stadium (Butts Road). This is a brand new stadium you see

today, home of Coventry's Rugby team. A fabled reunion concert by The Specials to open the new stadium (to coincide with the band's 25th Anniversary) was mooted around for several months. In 1981 when racial tension in Britain was at a high, a Festival against Racism was organised by Jerry Dammers on June 20th 1981, (Dammers had been primarily motivated after seeing an Asian doctor Amal Dharry stabbed to death at his local fish and chip shop in Broomfield Rd). It was to be an all day charity concert held at the Butts Stadium. The line up that day was The People, The Bureau, The Reluctant Stereotypes, Hazel O'Connor and The Specials. "The biggest thrill for me as a performer", said Hazel O'Connor. "Was playing alongside The Specials at The Butts when in spite of threats from the misanthropic right - a wonderful concert took place and people came out to show solidarity against the racist climate of that time". The New National Front picked that day to march in the City and some Earlsdon residents fought tooth and nail to get the concert cancelled, but despite the rain and the poor turn-out it proved a great day for local music and local common sense. I was just glad to have been there.

(14) The Butts Technical College (Butts Road). A place of learning by

day and entertainment at night. It was here that Horace, Jerry and Neol would watch artists like the Average White Band and ultimate reggae band Misty In Roots (originally Nicky Thomas's backing band). Neol also got to play here with his short-lived project named Castrovalva (named after a M. C. Escher lithograph).

DOUBLE 'A' SIDE SINGLE

Ghost Town

c/w **Why?**

Friday Night Saturday Morning

AVAILABLE IN 7 AND 12

MARKETED BY CHRYSALIS RECORDS LTD.

SATURDAY NIGHT FEVER '81 STYLE ... LIVE!

SAT. 20 JUNE COVENTRY Butts Athletic Stadium
Special Guests Hazel O'Connor · The Bureau ·
Reluctant Stereotypes · The People
A PEACEFUL PROTEST AGAINST RACISM

Above right, The Butts Technical College. Above right, part of the advert for Ghost Town, including details of the Butts gig. Bottom Terry, Lynval and Jerry at the Butts. Photo by John Coles.

At the side of the Butts Technical College turn into Albany Road, carry on under the bridge on the left hand side you will find number 51. Please do not disturb the current tenants .

51 Albany Road

The spiritual home of 2 Tone, and Jerry Dammers then humble dwelling. The band rehearsed and partied here and used it as the 2 Tone office. A BBC2 Arena TV special was aired during the height of 2 Tone, it was an over-view of the Specials hosted by Adrian Thrills. With much footage shot at Albany Road, It showed The Specials and The Selecter partying (or pretending to) and Jerry emptying the demo tapes they had been sent from their 2-Tone A&R department (well actually just a drawer)! Some of the Gangsters singles were rubber stamped here and Neol Davies created his own limited edition collector's item that reads "The Selecter VS The Special AKA Gangsters" as opposed to the 'normal' other way around (coming to an e-bay site near you soon)! It was here that Jerry constructed the original Selecter poster taken from a photo shot under the fly-over opposite The Old Fire Station in Coventry. The montage took hours to cut by hand and lay out, on near completion Jerry's faithful dog came along and destroyed the whole thing resulting in even more hours work!

51 Albany Road, outside and inside, photo courtesy of the BBC.

Neville Staples once owned a house nearby in Broomfield Road in 1980. The flat was also home to Chris Dickie, bass player with the hyper-inventive Coventry band Gods Toys. I asked Roddy about Jerry's then home, the answer wasn't very flattering. " We had the BBC filming us while we were recording for the Arena documentary. I remember Jerry's flat was always a tip! They tided it up for the documentary and put posters and pictures up and a clothes rail (that fell down during filming), so it looked like somebody actually lived there! But it was more like a tramp's squat normally". While Lynval looked at the house in a more catalytic way, "51 Albany Road, home of 2 Tone, the best record label ever. Whilst other record companies were taking things seriously we were having fun and releasing records that spoke on behalf of the youth of that generation". The flat is now looking very smart by the way, and the current residents were totally unaware and surprised on hearing of the flats chequered past!

ackson, the barbers was next door to Jerry's flat. They were filmed here
s part of the Arena documentary. Although it never made It to the final cut.
`his still photograph was by Brian Griffin.

Below, Roddy filming with Ben Sidwell at 2-Tone HQ, in Albany Road for the
BBC.

Retrace steps back to end of Albany Road. Turn right towards City. (Close by is Upper York St home of The Glasshouse and Queens Rd location of a multi-storey car park where the earliest Automatics/Specials photos were taken). Continue back through subway (underpass), (nearby is where The Nerve Boutique used to stand). Cross over to Iceland Store, carry on left towards St Johns Church. Turn in through glass doors to Lower Precinct, take escalator on right up to second floor for T.J. Hughes this was Mr George's nightclub.

(16) Mr George's Nightclub (Lower Precinct).

The department store T.J Hughes now stands on the site of this popular nightclub. The Sex Pistols Played here on the 17th December 1977, They had created much 'negative' publicity in the press. So they went incognito as The S.P.O.T.S (Sex Pistols On Tour Secretly). The Automatics approached the band for the support slot but roadies Steve English & Rodent told them to go away! The Automatics did however gain a Monday night residency here from Jan to April 1978. According to Terry Hall the place was full of teddy boys. By March they had become The Coventry Automatics. Lynval sees it like this, " Mr George, The best gig, the best crowd, the best beer..oh wait, the best beer was at the Domino. Mr Georges, not all the girls were slags but the beer did taste like….."

Above Mr George, and Right entrance to the Domino!

Continue around on balcony, look for Lush the new-age soap shop (with the stylised neon racing cars above). Lush and the story above (and above Dorothy Perkins) was the location of The Domino Restaurant

(17) The Domino Restaurant (Lower Precinct)

This is where Jerry one night asked Roddy to join the Specials. Indeed the next day a rather hung-over Roddy was awoken by Jerry Dammers and Pete Waterman hammering at his front door, eager to get to London to record a demo tape (the songs recorded were: Jaywalker, Too Much Too Young, Little Bitch and Dawning Of A New Era.) Lynval reveals it was a favourite of his "Late nights at The Domino doing what all the youth would do at that time of night, drinking beer, getting drunk and chasing girls". The Specials played here on 5th December 1978.

THE SPECIALS

lightening tour of coventry
thurs 30 nov dog & trumpet
fri 1 dec hand & hart
tues 5 dec domino

Above left, an early poster showing gigs at The Domino,The Dog & Trumpet and the Hand & Heart. Above right, The Specials on the roof of the Queens Rd car park Earsldon(now part of the Ramada Hotel complex).

The picture centre left is the car park as it stands today. Bottom left, a third shot from the Queens Rd session, taken from the opposite wall of the car park looking towards the City centre. On the left is the long gone GEC building, (now site of the Sky Dome), and on the extreme right is the Market clock tower. This and the above right photo were used on the inside cover front cover respectively of the Coventry Automatics CD "Dawning Of A New Era". Photos copyright of Jeff Veitch, poster from Roddy's private collection.

"I took those photos many, many moons ago, while studying Fine Art at the Lanch - on the same course as Jerry, Horace and Brad. When the Automatics/Specials got going, I was learning photography and would work for beer, so I ended up taking quite a lot of 2 tone related pix" - Jeff Veitch.

Go down steps to ground level, turn left at Waterstones Bookshop (who sell my books) to find Central Library ahead.

(18) Tiffany's (The Precinct)

As a venue in the city, it was only second to that of Coventry Theatre. With its strange glass entrance tower dominating the City's Precinct (sadly now of course gone, when the main building became the home of the new central library), a good night was pretty much guaranteed for all. The revolving stage turning to the sound of Green Onions is a powerful memory for many. So was Pete Watermans DJ stints at the venue. The Automatics (3-1-78),The Specials (29-5-79 & 20-12-79), The Selecter (29-5-79 & 20-3-80), The Beat (20-12-79) Madness (24-4-80)and The Swinging Cats and The Bodysnatchers (both 20-3-80) all graced the stage here. The Specials recorded the B side of their number one *Special AKA live EP* here. The City was never quite the same when it was closed down. Some of the things recorded at Tiff's include The B side of the Specials AKA Live EP, the Skinhead Symphony. Also recorded on the same night was The Selecter's Carry Go Bring Home, B-side of Missing Words single, it also made it's way onto the US issue off Dance Craze LP. Chuck Berry recorded one side of his London Sessions LP here including the number one single My Ding A-Ling. Fittingly It is hoped that there will be a commemorative plaque erected here at some point dedicated to that wonderful Coventry invention; 2-Tone music!

Coventry's Precinct was also featured in the BBC Arena documentary of The Specials phenomenon as the setting for Concrete Jungle and Blank Expression. It was also in the Precinct that the racial seeds of unrest were apparent in the early 80's with the gathering of Police and Asian youths protesting at racially motivated attacks. More recently Horace Panter has played open air concerts here with his bands the Coventry Ska Jazz Orchestra and the Coventry Semi-Automatics as part of Coventry's prestige Jazz Festival. It was also the location of yet another Specials photograph.

Above, Tiff's From inside (as used on the rear of the Too Much, Too Young live EP cover from the Coventry Telegraph) and right Terry Hall and Two Tone fan in Tiffs 1980 Photo by Angela Kerrigan

Above left, Suggs and fans (Pauline & Shelia) at Tiffany's 1980, thanks to Shelia Kerrigan. Above right Tiff's circa 1980.

Below Charlie of the Selecter at the rear of Tiffany's with fans, photo courtesy of Toni Tye (the young chap at the front is probably saying, "You ain't seen me-right").

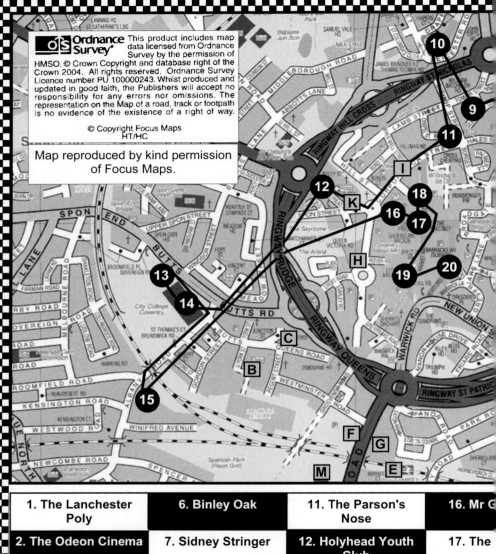

1. The Lanchester Poly	6. Binley Oak	11. The Parson's Nose	16. Mr G
2. The Odeon Cinema	7. Sidney Stringer	12. Holyhead Youth Club	17. The
3. The Oak Inn	8. The Tic Toc Club	13. Butts Stadium	18. Ti
4. Far Gosford Street	9. The City Centre Club	14. Butts Tech	19. Virgin
5. Lucas Aerospace	10. Canal Basin	15. 51 Albany Road	20. The Tru

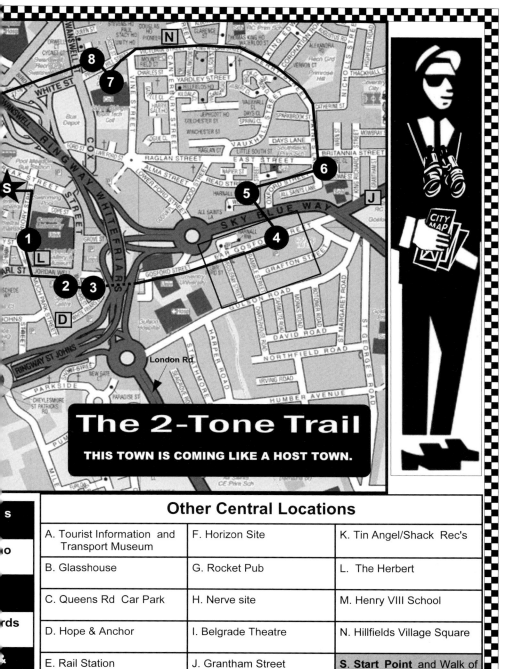

The 2-Tone Trail

THIS TOWN IS COMING LIKE A HOST TOWN.

Other Central Locations

A. Tourist Information and Transport Museum	F. Horizon Site	K. Tin Angel/Shack Rec's
B. Glasshouse	G. Rocket Pub	L. The Herbert
C. Queens Rd Car Park	H. Nerve site	M. Henry VIII School
D. Hope & Anchor	I. Belgrade Theatre	N. Hillfields Village Square
E. Rail Station	J. Grantham Street	**S. Start Point** and Walk of Fame site (Specials Star)

From Library head back towards Waterstones Bookshop, keep straight on towards the high-rise block past Market Way and Sheldon Square into City Arcade. The first shop you will see in the arcade is The Liquid Café Wine Bar, this was originally Virgin Records.

(19) **Virgin Records** (City Arcade) Brad of the Specials worked here as did Chris Long of The Swinging Cats and Tim Strickland who was briefly in The Coventry Automatics (they both later ran *Inferno Records* together in the Precinct). Meanwhile Pete Waterman(a one-time Specials manager) had the upstairs known as The Soul Hole. Apparently a young Simon Mayo queued up here to buy his copy of Gangsters, when he attended Warwick University. The Specials first album also did well at Virgin selling over 300 copies on the day of it's release, this was repeated at other Coventry record shops like Jill Hansons, W.H. Smiths and HMV.

Right: An archive photo outside Virgin from the rather original and brilliant Cov fanzine Alternative Sounds , run by the legendary Martin Bowes. The zine' covered (amongst loads of other stuff) a lot of the Specials activities, thank goodness we all say.

Retrace your steps, turn right at Card Warehouse into Sheldon Square then go straight into the Bull Yard and turn left into Hertford St pedestrian street. Continue onto The Dog and Trumpet on left.

(20) **The Dog and Trumpet** (Hertford Street) A subterranean pub that began life as a Beer Keller and became a major venue in the town. The newly named Specials played here on Thursday 30th November 1978. Bad Manners played here a few times, as did General Public who included former 2-Tone troopers, Horace Panter from the Specials, Dave Wakeling and Ranking Roger from the Beat as well as Micky Billingham from Dexy's Midnight Runners. On a personal note it was here (my diary says 22nd August 1979), Jerry Dammers talked me into giving him my precious Coventry Rude Boy badge; well I had another one! This venue has recently enjoyed a revamp, and has come back stronger and better.

The multi-talented Horace with General Public at The Dog & Trumpet.

Above right The Dog and Trumpet, left Dave Wakeling of General Public playing at the Dog! Right that Ska badge.

That concludes the main part of the 2-Tone Trail. It also leaves you right in the middle of Coventry City centre. Heading back in the direction you came will lead you to Coventry Railway Station. Or if you carry on straight you will come to Broadgate from here you can head back to the Transport Museum.

If you did the tour thanks, and we hope you enjoyed it! If you have any comments or suggestions for the tour, I can be contacted at **2-tone@covmusic.net** *Pete Chambers.*

Out Of Town Sites

These sites are off the main core trail because of their considerable distance from Coventry City Centre.

The Bantam (Hen Lane) used by Night Train for their rehearsals, the band included Jerry Dammers and Neol Davies.

Broad Street Producer Roger Lomas had built a four-track studio in his Broad Street garden. He got a visit from a certain Neol Davies with an idea for a new song, it was duly recorded and the track (The Kingston Affair) would eventually re-surface as The Selecter and grace the B-side of The Specials (and 2 Tone) first single Gangsters. It would also pave the way for Neol to form a band around the name The Selecter. From then on Roger became 'the man' when it came to producing 2-Tone. He became the 'In-House' Producer at Coventry's Horizon Studios. Roger Lomas, "My studio in Broad Street was at number 46 and was just a small 4 track studio but I still managed to get some good recordings out of it".

Burnaby Road, A street in the Radford area of the City. Former Specials drummer Silverton lived here, his house was used by The Coventry Automatics to rehearse. Jerry and Brad also lived in this road. The public house The Pilot is also in Burnaby Road. In the mid seventies Neol Davies and Brad ran the Hollywood Jazz Club upstairs here, As Neol puts it, "It was a desperate an ultimately ill-fated attempt at making our own amusement. We even tried our hand at jazz improv'...nice!". Jerry Dammers also came here to check out Lynval and Silverton's band Pharoah's Kingdom.

Fisher Road Neol Davies was born here on April 26th 1952. "I was born right behind the Heath Hotel in Fisher Road" Said Neol, "as was Silverton who became the Specials original drummer".

The General Wolfe (Foleshill Road) The Specials rehearsed the routine for the Ghost Town video here, and The Selecter also rehearsed here. it was normal to spot a least one Special here on a gig night. The Wolfe was a major Coventry venue for local talent probably the most important rock venue in the City. Indeed when Visit Britain published their England Rocks map in 2007, Coventry only got two mentions, one for 2-Tone, and the other for The General Wolfe! One name springs to mind when you talk about the Wolfe that's Ken Brown. Ken's a convivial bloke from Enniskillen, and a huge Van Morrison fan, and a 'king' in the promotion of local talent. His importance on the local scene can not be overstated. His long stint at the 'Wolf' saw a plethora of bands on its small but perfectly formed stage (even U2 played there in September 1980). Ken Brown, "We used to have two West Indian guys who used to play blue beat at the Wolfe, funny enough they had the same surname as me Brown. They were the Brown Brothers. They were very secretive of their music they never let anyone find out who it was, because they wanted to keep it to themselves. So obviously Jerry (Dammers) and the boys were heavily influenced by that adding their own punk and rock elements to it. The Wolfe recently began rocking again and thanks to manager Bob Davidson, it boasts a "Wall of Fame", and thanks to Aitch Bembridge, an area dedicated to Two Tone.

Out Of Town Sites Continued

The Heath Hotel (Foleshill Road). The Automatics had a residency at the Heath from October 1977 and rumour has it that they also recorded a live demo tape here. This was where they also made their debut under the name The Specials in 1978. Jerry Dammers remembers that it was so cold here that they would light a fire and frequently gather firewood, "I've no idea where the firewood came from", Jerry reveals. It wasn't just cold though, it was small too, I had to play with my back to the crowd because I couldn't fit my organ on the stage (no tittering at the back). Ironically it's now a reggae venue called *Club re*.

London Road Abbey Court flats are located along The London Road. In the late seventies they were home to The Specials Bassman Horace Panter. It was here where 5,000 white sleeves for the Gangsters single were hand stamped by Horace and Terry Hall. Further along the road is Cabin Studios. One time Reluctant Stereotype who supported The Specials) Paul Sampson was the in-house producer there, ran the place looking after the likes of Sonic Boom, The Primitives, Catatonia and lots of other demo stuff.

Above: Wolfe manager Bob Davidson and the 2-Tone Wall.

Left, The General Wolfe Foleshill Rd

Out Of Coventry

Midland Sound Recorders (Meeting House Lane, Balsall Common) It was here Neol Davies had an Acetate of The Selecter (The Kingston Affair) cut, this song was to eventually turn up as the B side of Gangsters.

The Regent Hotel (The Parade, Leamington Spa). The location of the 'cocktail lounge cover of the More Specials album. Roddy " Yeah it was the back room, I think Jerry had discovered it on his travels. I remember a Cov girl fan came along to add a bit of vavoom Apart from that it was pretty boring like most photo shoots". "For the second cover" ,photographer Chalkie Davies recalls, "Jerry wanted a Jazz sleeve feel to it, it's taken in a bar in Leamington Spa. We took the Polaroids and Jerry just wanted to finish i there and then. He was completely happy with them, because he wanted the people out of focus. We shot a very similar picture for the American market (as used in the poster tha came with the British version).

Rugby Town– Neville Staple grew up in this Warwickshire Town.

Woodbine Studios (Woodbine Street, Leamington Spa). It was here that Ghost Town (and it's B-sides) were recorded, in an eleven day session. Engineered by house producer (and studio owner) Johnny Rivers, he remembers it like this. "That song still stands up as the best 8-track recording I have ever heard, though the whole thing would have been nothing without Horace and Brad's rhythm section. In my opinion Horace is one of the world's bes three bass players!" Much of The Specials AKA In The Studio album was recorded at the new Woodbine studio in St Mary's Road.

The Regent Hotel Leamington as seen on the UK cover of More Specials. With the rare third alternative cassette cover photo above right. Left, Terry Hall, another rare portrait from the More album Regent photo sessions.

ther related sites

ob Armstrong, top class guitar maker, who lives in the Stoke area of Coventry. He once ʰade a fretless bass for Mark 'Bedders' Bedford of Madness.

elgrade Theatre, This was the venue in September 2000 & May 2001 for the 2-Tone ʰfluenced stage show Three-minute Hero. Written by Bob Eaton and starring Coventrian ⁿdi Smith the show was set in Coventry's Precinct circa 1979-81, and it tells a fictitious ᵒry of five youngsters and their music, it also featured some twenty ska classics. Other ᵊttings featured The Lanch and the Pioneer House tower block in Adelaide St, Hillfields ᵉol Davis played a solo concert here in November 1975 using multi-tracked backing ʰpes, but never liked the solitude of the solo performance.

anley College, An early venue for the Coventry Automatics.

oventry Transport Museum (Millennium Place). You can listen to Ghost Town playing ᵊre on a display that outlines the sad decline of motor manufacturing in the area. It can be ʰund on the first floor, and some of the songs lyrics are also on display.

he Coventry Theatre (Coventry Hippodrome). A major player for rock and pop music in ᵉ City, but has very little 2-Tone connection. Although The Selecter's Neol Davies ᶦtnessed Jimi Hendrix here and went deaf for three days before realising music was the ᵃth for him! The Millennium clock now occupies the space left ⱱ the theatre.

avid Fletcher Ltd (Station Square), Terry Hall worked here ʰhen It was a coin dealers. It would seem that numismatism ʷas not the career for him. It actually got a mention on the back ᵒver of Too Much Too Young EP. It's now a post office. Further ᵈwn the row of shops is Loafers, sadly just a batch bar Oppo-ʰte is Coventry Railway Station site of another set of Specials ʳomotion pictures.

arlsdon Birthplace of Roderick James Byers on 5/5/55 and ᵒme for many years for Jerry Dammers. Also the location of ᵉ Butts stadium, Butts College & 2-Tone HQ..

host Town (Coventry?). Well was it about Coventry? Well ᵊs, but not just Coventry. The initial inspiration was according Jerry Dammers an area of Glasgow (many claim the area to ᵊ Easterhouse, but Jerry tells me he's never been specific on that one). The fact is the ᵒng was really an indictment to many areas in many cities and towns of the time.

**Terry At Cov Station
Photo Joe Kerrigan**

ʰe Glasshouse (Upper York Street) Opening in 1982, this education based audio re-ᵒrding facility was set up by Charlie Anderson, and former Hardtop 22 man Amos Ander-ᵒn (who would become the director of the facility). It offers courses in production, sound ⁿgineering, video production and even promotion, with 'Democracy' being the in house cord label. In Summer 2005 a re-formed Selecter (without Neol or Pauline) recorded ᵊre.

Green Lane Underpass Murals

If you venture out of the city just a few yards on from the Burnt Post public house, you will come to Green Lane. It's here you will find Green Lane Subway which runs under the A45 (Kenpass Highway). Down the underpass and you will be greeted with many famous Cov entry people and places. First the actor Clive Owen and as you turn into the subway proper seven Cov lads that shook the world. The Specials of course, based on the famous 'skyscraper' promo shot, that Nev tells me was taken in the Heath Hotel.

It's a good place to pose between the murals of the band and the one that says 'The Specials', be warned though, it's a bugger to photograph without getting reflection from the lights in it. Other murals depict The Italian Job and the Coventry Blitz. A similar piece of "Specials" (and The Enemy) Urban art can be seen in the City Centre pub the Golden Cross.

ther related sites continued

rantham St, Brad lived in this street for many years opposite Gosford Green park in the toke district of Coventry, he also attended Binley Park School.

he Herbert Arts, Media, Museum, History Centre (Jordan Well) Was once home to a nall display of 2-Tone items donated by various Specials, In 2008, the Herbert will in- ude many 2-Tone items in it's new gallery space. In 2009, a Coventry Music exhibition, ovisionally titled 'Not Just Two Tones', will celebrate 2-Tone in Style.

he Hope and Anchor, (Whitefriars Street) like it's much higher profiled London name- ke, this pub was the watering hole for the local muso scene. Full to the rafters with ace cadets and those who would given time 'make a difference'. A sort of 2-Tone Gentle- an's club. The Swinging Cats played here a fair bit and their vocalist Chris Long (Craig uatemala) was the resident DJ. I asked former Swinging Cat Jane Bayley/Jayne De la wing or Jane Bom-Bane if she remembered 2-Tone Coventry? "I remember the Hope and nchor very well and played there several times with the Swinging Cats. Did you know that Tone Tess, who ran the Specials fan club from the Specials office near Livingstone wimming Baths, is Leigh my sister"! In 2007, the pub shone again as the spiritual home of die band The Enemy.

FREE!
LUNCHTIME
CONCERT
NEOL DAVIES
GUITAR electric & acoustic
with multi-track tape accompani- ment recorded by himself

FRIDAY NOV 29 1.15
ON STAGE AT THE
BELGRADE
AR OPEN 12–2
NACKS

ight former Selecter Charley Anderson at e Glasshouse and above right The oventry Automatics circa 1978 at Canley ollege, above left, a poster from Neol avies private collection.

Other related sites continued

Horizon Studios (Warwick Road). Is a major 2-Tone site, though sadly now part of The Central Six shopping complex (well the entrance road at least), and although it isn't on the actual trail, it's worth a few pages to itself. It was probably one of the most well known studios in the area, The Specials, the Selecter made their historic 2 Tone albums here. Other artists like Bad Manners, The Three Degrees and Steel Pulse have all used the now long gone Warwick Road 24 track. It was probably the most tangible face of 2 Tone in the city. Studio costs were £20 an hour plus VAT in 1980.

"I remember Barry the owner got us all into his office to give us a telling off", says Roddy, had carved my name into a wooden ash tray stand and Terry had slashed a arm chair! We thought it was pretty funny considering the amount of money we were paying him". Over to Roger Lomas, "I quite enjoyed working in Horizon Studios, It was a friendly, homely sort of atmosphere. I produced The Selecter's 2nd album there (Celebrate The Bullet), Bad Manners first two albums (Ska'n'B & Loonee Tunes), The Modettes album, Reluctant Stereotypes album & singles. 'Hit' singles I produced at Horizon were: On My Radio, Missing Words and The Whisper" (The Selecter). Special Brew, Lorraine and Just A Feeling (Bad Manners)". The Beat came to record Tears of a Clown and Ranking Full Stop, here but because of technical problems and the fact they weren't keen to sound like other 2-tones bands left with just a half recorded version of Ranking Full Stop. They eventually finished the single's two sides in London.

"The best thing about Horizon Studios was it was within walking distance from my house and the city centre". Explains Pauline Black. "Which made it very convenient. In 1980, remember leaving Horizon Studio, where we were recording our fourth single 'The Whisper' and popping down to the Registry Office in Coventry to marry my husband during his lunch hour. We used our two roadies as witnesses. After the brief ceremony, my husband went back to work and I went back to lay down my vocal track!"

Top, In Horizon Studios, recording the first album. Below outside the florists that stood opposite the studio, and indeed still stands opposite the former site. Photos by Jeff Veitch

Top, now you see the Horizon building, Below, now you don't. Good to see that the Rocket Pub is still standing though.

Speaking of the Rocket, below, Rodd and Nev in the very same pub, about to do a piece to camera.

Below another rare Chalkie Davies pic of Horace and Lynval in the Rocket with Chrissie Hynde circa 1979

Keresley, is it a village, is it an area of Coventry? One thing's for sure Roddy Byers grew up here.

King Henry VIII School, (Warwick Road) Just up a little from where Horizon Studios stood you will find King Henry VIII, one of Coventry's top schools and the one Jerry Dammers attended.

Nerve Boutique (69, Queen Victoria Road) "The shop was started by Clare (my Wife) in 1981". Reveals Horace, "and I joined her as part of my 'rock'n'roll de-compression' strategy after being totally fed up with music after I left the Specials in the spring of 1982. We went from just a small lock-up shop to do manufacturing as well. We created our own logo-brand clothes and accessories and ended up employing 3 people in a council-sponsored industrial unit in Alderman's Green as well as one full-time shop assistant. Nerve clothes were sold all over the country for a while in 1983/4. Clare eventually sold the shop to Chris Long (of the Swinging Cats) in 1984. He moved the premises to Corporation Street, opposite what used to be the Tally Ho. By that time I was commuting to Birmingham to work with Dave Wakeling and Ranking Roger in General Public". The Ikea complex now stands where the shop used to be. Just up the road from Nerve. Stood **The Drill Hall** a large old building used for local groups and organisations. Many fought to save it including The Specials, especially Roddy Byers and Horace Panter. Roddy's band the Tearjerkers took part in a concert at The Butts College to save the hall, 21 Guns (who were signed to Neville's Shack Records) were also on the Bill. The Hall went the same way as Nerve sadly and was demolished to became part of the new Co-op complex, that was demolished to become part of the Ikea complex!

Above left, the Nerve boutique, and right the Tin Angel as it stands now, once part of Neville Staples empire, namely Shack Records HQ.

Planet Studios, Cash's Lane, Foleshill, a favourite with the mark II Specials and Neville Staple.

Regent Street, situated in Earlsdon, number 7 was the one time home of both Jerry and Horace. "I lived there from 1976 until 1978" Horace says," After I moved on to Abbey Court, Jerry had the place until he moved to Albany Road. The photo (see below) is of a rehearsal we held there, probably in '78', around the time of the Clash tour".

Rose Inn, now the defunct Lockhurst Tavern on Lockhurst Lane. The reformed Specials played here on three occasions between 97/98, and it only cost £3.00 to get in!

pon Street, Above what is now The Tin Angel bar and venue, was Neville Staple headuarters for his Shack records project.

Valsgrave Hospital, the Selecter's Pauline Black worked here as a radiographer after rst qualifying at the City's Coventry & Varwickshire Hospital.

Varwick University, The Specials layed a Rock Against Racism gig here n 19th Feb 1978, supported by Gods oys and Terry's old band Squad. Hardp 22 played the venue later on the 24th eb also 1978.

he Whitley Abbey Pub, Close to lorace's then home and the scene of hany various gigs by many various ands including The Mosquitoes, and The 1ix. I remember seeing Lynval in the udience there one night and I am proud o say I shared the stage with Horace nd Neol Davies, I must have made an npact as Neol has no recollection of the ig at all!

he Special Mk II, Roddy and Aitch laying at The Rose Inn. Don't eem right to me?

hoto Joe Kerrigan

Taking the Trail

Since the 2-Tone trail began in 2005, there has been interest from all quarters. The Trail even got onto CV One's (the City Centre management Company) Media tour page of it's website. It has sold in the following countries; Britain, Ireland, France, Germany, Holland, Australia, USA, Hong Kong, Canada, Austria, Spain, Hungary & Sweden. Various Rudy types have come to 'the Motherland' Coventry to do the trail around the city. I managed to collar some folks to give me an insight into their tour experiences. Here are a few.

Julian McKenzie– a writer from Sheffield, and author of the book, 'Well tonight Matthew, I'm Gonna' Be A Rude Boy'.

Whoever it was who proclaimed there's no point in dwelling in the past, obviously had no knowledge of the impact that 2-tone would have on so many musical lives. My name is Julian McKenzie, a writer from Sheffield, and ever since The Specials debut single collided head on into my life at the tender age of ten, I've had black and white blood flowing freely through my veins. And now thirty years on, and a new title to my name (that of forty-something) the hangover continues. From the moment I fell down the stairs of the Dog and Trumpet (I was sober honest!) to the Lanchester Polytechnic (yes I did the tour backwards) I got a sense of what it was like in those heady days of conception and birth of 2-tone. When doing the tour that Pete meticulously created, I took time out to pause for a few seconds outside each individual site. Butts, Tiffany's, Tic Toc, the canal basin the list is endless, I also tried to generate the atmosphere of yesteryear, and believe me when you've combined that to your tour will become a magical one.

Julian McKenzie

On a personal note I thoroughly enjoyed each individual moment, and although my sense of direction is about as handy as one of those high tech sat nav thingamabobs, I'd like to think I didn't miss any of the sites highlighted in the book. Chambers has his finger firmly on the pulse, his attention to detail in making this an enjoyable and pleasurable step back in time is second to none. As far as recommendations go, it's a must. You may not have been there in the beginning, but what a unique opportunity to catch up!

Mike Cornwell-Ska and 2-Tone fan extraordinaire

Being a fan of The Specials and all things 2 Tone from the age of nine,I had always wanted to see the places that were part of the making of 2 Tone history, So when the book The 2 Tone Trail ' came out I had to buy it and take part .So on a cold February day in 2006 I set out from the Lanchester Polytechnic. I had a great time visiting all these important places on route, the best parts for me were 51 Albany Road the 2 tone headquarters ,the canal basin where the photo shoots for 'More Specials' took place and 'Tiffany's' where the b side of the live EP was recorded. Overall the trail is a must for any die hard or up and coming 2 Tone fan, very educational and most enjoyable trip. I highly recommend you take the time and have a visit.

You see before you two of the toppest ska fans on this planet. That's Paul Willo' Williams on the left and Mike Cornwell on the right, where would the fandom be without these guys? Huge respect.

LOOSE ENDS AND THANKS

There are some people whose input was above and beyond the call of duty, they are Lynval Golding, Horace Panter, Roddy Byers, Jerry Dammers, Roger Lomas, Pauline Black, Steve Blackwell, Paul Williams, Mike Cornwell, Focus Maps, Simon Kelly, Simon Ward, Darrell and Special Brew. Pete Walters at CV One, Roger Vaughan at Coventry City Council and not forgetting Lynval & Neol for their excellent forewords. Huge thanks to the following for the use of their photos. John Coles, Toni Tye, The Coventry Evening Telegraph, Alex Ogg, EMI Publishing Ltd, Jeff Veitch, Paul Williams, Joe, Angela and Sheila Kerrigan, ITV Central News, Dave McGrory, Hannah Tobin, and Chalkie Davies & Carol Starr. Lots of other thanks to, Neville Staple, Professor Anthony Lis, Bob Brolly and BBC Coventry & Warwickshire, Ray King, Claire Hope, Gaps, Anthony Harty, Jane Bom-Bane, Kev Monks, Paul Heskett, Ali Bushnell, Nick Stokes, Andrew Green, Michelle Golding, John Dawkins, The Enemy, the Ripps, Q Magazine and Johnny Black for their 2-Tone Maps and Legend article, Paul Heller . Plus a special thank you to my wife Julie for all her help & support and a huge bunch of thanks to Tony Beard, Coventry University, The Herbert and Brian and Bill and all the gang at Coventry Market for their huge support.

Contact me at **2-tone-2@covmusic.net** or at the websites
www.myspace.com/2tonetwo and **www.2-tone-2.synthasite.com**

Websites you really must check out.

The definitive Specials website, run by Miles Woodroffe **www.thespecials.com/**

This is the bible when it comes to 2-Tone records, wonderful stuff, visit
Jason & Peter at **http://2-tone.info/**

The Specials (unofficial fans page) **www.myspace.com/thespecialsfans**

Radiate to the World of Roddy, a fascinating site **www.roddyradiation.com**

Neville Staple Myspace **www.myspace.com/nevillestaplefromthespecials**

Neol Davies's Myspace **www.myspace.com/neoldavies**

Special Brew's Myspace **www.myspace.com/specialbrewinfo**

Paul Williams Myspace **www.myspace.com/paulwillo**

Mikes Cornwell's Myspace **www.myspace.com/mikecornwell**

The Selecter **www.theselecter.net**

Every effort has been made to trace the copyright holders of all the photographs used in this book, but one or two have proved unreachable, and we apologise if any photographs have gone unaccredited.

I would like to give huge thanks to all our advertisers and major sponsors like my good friend and all round good guy Tony Beard and the Herbert, and it's spectacular new development, that undoubtedly will be something to be proud of, and of course our main sponsor Coventry Market. Like 2-Tone, you really can't separate the market from the City where it belongs. My thanks go out to all who help animate that special place we call Coventry market and especially Market Manager Brian Sexton, who has been a joy to work with on this project. Next year 2-Tone will be 30 years old, this year the market celebrates its 50th. Here are some of my observations on this other Cov icon.

If you are from Cov, then you love the market, I don't know how that works but it just does. Shops and stores come and go, but the market remains at the heart of Coventry shopping. I would love a pound every time I have heard the phrase, "Have you tried Coventry market". For me the market has always just been there, like many other Coventry youngsters a special treat was to ride on the roundabout by the outside cafe. We often take this large round concrete structure for granted, but if they ever demolish it, you can bet the local media will have a field-day with disgruntled Cov-kids horrified by such a proposal. "Its just a market", some will say, well on many levels it is. Though on others, it's far more than that, its unique, it has its own feel about it, it's own smell (and I'm not just talking about the Fish mongers here).

The place is alive, organic if you will, like any place worth spending time in, it's the people that make it. The building may stand as a reminder of Coventry's post war resurgence and ability to adapt, but without a steady stream of Coventrians and the like it remains a hollow shell. Everyone who has lived in the area for any length of time has at least one memory of this place, more often or not a story. I can remember as a young child, that much like the above mentioned Roundabout treat, when you got into the market, you seemed to be moving round and around for ever. Eventually getting back to where you had started, I could never work it out as a child, even today, I probably couldn't tell you where you would end up if you headed in a forward direction at any given location. That was always the fun though, this big round concrete place, full of people usually quite animated (especially the stall holders), it was an exciting place to visit as a child.

As a young teenager I was a part of the suede head set, suede heads were basically skinheads who's parents wouldn't let them have a number one haircut. My Saturday morning ritual in the early 1970's, was to cycle into town to the market. Go and buy my yellow and red Brutus check shirt, or maybe some red socks or a tiepin for my crombie overcoat. Then hope your bike was where you left it, cycle back home and get your new clobber ready for the disco that night. The market never seems to let you down, you could (and still can) get everything here and more often than not it was cheaper too, and the people watching is pretty good too!

I suppose market shopping was always a little different to conventional retail therapy. Cov Market unlike most stores, has atmosphere and life and interaction is always encouraged. Because this is not just your average market, no this is Coventry Market, I'm mighty glad it's ours.

So next time you venture to Coventry, after you have sampled the delights of the Cathedral, the Herbert, and of course the 2-Tone Trail, you may want to head down to the market, a fine way to find out what makes us Coventry folk tick!

Pete's next book project will be the history of the Coventry Market, as commissioned by Coventry Market, to be published late 2009.

The market Roundabout

COVENTRY MARKET
1958-2008

"If you are from Coventry, then you love the market, I don't know how that works but it just does. Shops and stores come and go, but the market remains at the heart of Coventry shopping".
Pete Chambers

As always I am so grateful to my good friend Tony Beard and his generous sponsorship of this book and it's subsequent promotion. Tony is an active fund raiser for Coventry's own Myton Hospice project. He was keen to promote Myton Hospice and the growing fight against cancer in general. As well as losing his beloved wife Helen to the disease, he also recently lost good friend Rod Allen to it. Rod will be best remembered as the voice of the Fabulous Fortunes. It was Rod's vocals that gave an exciting epic feel to songs Like You've Got your Troubles and Here it Comes Again.

Rod Allen and Tony Beard

Myton Hospice Coventry Appeal

We are currently running a Capital Appeal to build a new hospice in Coventry. The hospice will be built on the site of the Walsgrave Hospital on Clifford Bridge Road. Although the building will be on an NHS site, the cost of building, equipping and the majority of running costs will be met through public donation. The Hospice will comprise a 20 bedded in patient unit with day hospice, counselling and lymphoedema services still under discussion.

If you think you can help then contact us at http://www.mytonhospice.org/

Or call us on 01926 492518 and ask for the Coventry Fundraising Team.

The Herbert

ARTS
MEDIA

OPENING TIMES MONDAY - SATURDAY 10AM - 5.30PM. SUNDAY 12 - 5PM

MUSEUM

The Herbert Jordan Well, Coventry, CV1 5QP. 024 7683 2386 www.theherbert.org

HISTORY

INCLUDES
HISTORY GALLERY MEDIEVAL, VICTORIAN AND 20TH CENTURY COVENTRY
DISCOVER GODIVA GALLERY
OLD MASTERS, SCULPTURE AND ART SINCE 1900
PEACE AND RECONCILIATION GALLERY
ELEMENTS NATURAL HISTORY GALLERY

The
Herbert

brownsindependentbar.com

A family owned and run bar.

Eat and drink all day and night.

Live visuals & dj's until 12am every Friday & Saturday night.

Live music venue.

Earl St, Coventry

Personality ARTISTES LTD

Presents

TONY "BANGER" WALSH

Brilliant After Dinner Speaker, Actor

STILL MINDING HIS OWN BUSINESS!!

An after dinner speaker you will not forget. Drawing on his many years as a former ITV "World of Sport" wrestling star and his subsequent career in the world of close protection, Tony is a guaranteed crowd puller!

PERSONALITY ARTISTES LTD

Worldwide Headquarters
PO Box 1 Blackpool
FY6 7WS United Kingdom
E-Mail: info@personalityartistes.com
www.personalityartistes.com

Contact Mal Ford
or Jean Parkes
Tel: +44(0)1253 899988
Fax: +44(0)1253 882823
www.malford.com

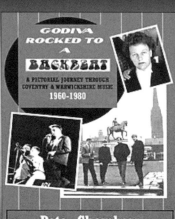

SHIMLA SPICE
CONTEMPORARY INDIAN CUISINE

Where a top class atmosphere matches a top quality meal, Shimla Spice the Midland's most elegant Indian Restaurant caters for all. Our top class chef will tantalise your tastebuds with an array of contemporary Indian cuisine. Why not try our **Shimla Spice Special** – all dishes are delicately cooked with freshly ground spices or even visit our spectacular 'eat as much as you like' Lunchtime Buffet.

With a fully licensed bar, full air-conditioning and relaxed surroundings, we guarantee your first experience will not be your last...

Opening Hours

Lunch	Monday - Saturday	12pm – 2.15pm
Evening	Sunday - Thursday	5.30pm – 11.45pm
Evening	Friday - Saturday	5.30pm – 12.30pm
	Sunday Lunch - *Closed*	

1 Copthall House • Station Square • Coventry • Telephone 024 7622 4085/4096

Specialising in Indian Wedding Receptions for upto 200 guests. Call us for an information pack.

THE NEW DOG & TRUMPET

HERTFORD STREET COVENTRY

FRIDAY NIGHTS
Indie, Dance, Drum & Bass, Cheese, Emo and DRINK PROMOTIONS

Free shot before 10.00pm

Free room for hire for private functions.

Carling just £1.90 Daytimes/Saturdays

Food available from 11.00am to 3.00pm

Tea and Coffee available

The New Dog & Trumpet is the last stop on the 2-Tone Trail. So when the your tour is over, why not join us for some refreshments, and soak up some of that old 2-Tone atmosphere!

57/97 Coventry Market, Queen Victoria Road, CV1 3HT, (024) 76 630 589

Dr Martens by Air Wear

14 Eye long-legs

8 Eye-boots

Yellow-stitch